BREAKTHROUGH!

DEVELOP THE 7 HABITS OF VICTORIOUS CHRISTIAN LIVING

By Jennifer LeClaire

Author of Fervent Faith and Doubtless

BREAKTHROUGH!

Unless otherwise noted, Scripture quotations are taken from the King James version of the Bible.

BREAKTHROUGH! The 7 Habits of Victorious Christian Living

Copyright © Jennifer LeClaire 2011

Published by Jennifer LeClaire Ministries

P.O. Box 3953

Hallandale Beach, Fla. 33008

305.467.4284

www.jenniferleclaire.org

DEDICATION

I dedicate this book to my beautiful daughter Bridgette, who motivated me to pick myself up and keep going despite the great odds against us.

TABLE OF CONTENTS

PREFACE

Stephen Covey has built a publishing empire on the back of his blockbuster bestseller "The 7 Habits of Highly Effective Living." There's "The 7 Habits of Highly Effective Teens," "The 7 Habits of Highly Effective Families," and, more recently, "The 8th Habit." In these books, Covey tells us to do things like be proactive, synergize, and sharpen the saw. All good advice.

Although we appreciate Covey's wisdom and brilliant book marketing strategies, let us not forget that the Bible has plenty of practical advice about good and bad habits alike. In fact, the Book of 2 Timothy, in particular, offers some nuggets of wisdom that describe what it takes to live a victorious Christian life—an abundant life that advances the Kingdom and glorifies God.

It should be duly noted that Paul's books (epistles) are bestsellers in their own right—they are chapters of the best-selling book of all time: the Bible. In 2 Timothy, a time-tested volume addressed to his young protégé, the Apostle Paul gives Timothy some final instructions. These instructions are the basis for the *Breakthrough!: The 7 Habits of Victorious Christian Living.*

I first stumbled upon this concept years ago while struggling to breakthrough the old man and its old ways. I was studying 2 Timothy, which is one of my favorite books in the Bible because it constantly encourages me to study the Word of God, to share what I've learned with others, to gently lead Gospel opponents to repentance, to fight the good fight of faith—and so much more.

Second Timothy contains some of Paul's famous last words. When someone is about to leave this earth, the last words they speak are worth noting. What did Paul say to Timothy in his last letter? What words did he leave the young pastor to exhort him in his personal fight of faith; a good fight that Paul himself fought and won? What did this great apostle share with Timothy about victorious Christian living?

Paul warned Timothy of some bad habits that would draw him away from his destiny, like idle talk that leads to ungodliness. He also warned him about the potentially deadly habits of being self-centered, greedy, proud, arrogant, disobedient, ungrateful, profane, slanderous, rash and treacherous, among others. But more than anything, Paul imparted some wise words that Timothy could refer back to long after his spiritual mentor went home to be with the Lord. These are what I like to call the *7 Habits of Victorious Christian Living*.

God offers the born-again believer an exciting walk with the Holy Spirit. It's not about liturgy. It's not about tradition. It's not about having your name on the church mailing list. It's about being out on the cutting edge, on the front line, and in the heat of the battle. It's about making a difference with your life by letting the Lord equip you, send you, and use you in a mighty way. Victorious Christian living demands discipline—good habits.

My prayer is that this book will serve as a reminder, even an inspiration, to follow Paul's instruction, because Paul followed Christ, he ran his race, and he finished his course. God saw it fit to leave a record of the habits Paul tried to instill in his spiritual sons, habits he no doubt lived out in his own life. Read this book with an open mind and a determined heart and you'll see transformation in areas of your life that you may not even have known needed transformed. You'll see stability. You'll see fruit that remains. You'll see victory, and you'll have the peace of God that passes all understanding once you master these habits by the grace of God.

INTRODUCTION

Victorious. Christian. Living. None of those words were part of my vocabulary when I was 30 years old. Breakthrough? No. Broke? Busted? Yes, and thoroughly disgusted with my lot in life.

Fast-forward 10 years and I'm living a victorious Christian life. It feels like a movie. I've got an intimate relationship with Jesus. I'm the single mother of a beautiful teenaged girl who loves the Lord. I'm on the editorial staff of *Charisma* magazine. And I've got bustling enterprises in the marketplace through which God supplies all my needs according to His riches in glory by Christ Jesus. I've found success, and more importantly significance. And I give God every ounce of the glory.

Indeed, I'm living out my passion day by day. I've written a number of Christian books. In fact, my materials have been translated into Spanish, Japan and Korean and some of my work is archived in the Flower Pentecostal Heritage Museum. It's all a dream come true. But it wasn't always that way.

Before I share with you *The 7 Habits of Victorious Christian Living* that totally transformed my life, I want to help you understand where I came from so you can see how far God has brought me. It might sound cliché, but He really has brought me from a mighty long way. And He did it, in part, by helping me develop the habits you'll read about on the pages of this book.

Let me encourage you with the condensed version of my testimony. I was born in 1970. My parents never exposed me to Jesus, at least not directly. I was a shy child, introverted, and one in whom the devil seemed to take an early interest. My life before Christ was marked by abuse, abandonment and plenty of pain. I spent the better part of two years during elementary school bedridden with a broken leg that required long-term traction followed by a body cast. I spent months virtually all alone watching reruns of "I Love Lucy," soap operas and cartoons.

This leg-breaking event happened two years in a row: two tractions, two body casts, two times learning how to walk again. I'm not sure if that event caused my introversion or just exacerbated it. But I never did absolutely fit in with any particular schoolyard clique. In high school I surrounded myself with misfits donning colored hair, if any, and black leather jackets complemented by high-cut Doc Martin boots.

Still, I went to church now and again with friends. I witnessed a Catholic Church mass one

Christmas. I went to a Presbyterian church on a military base one Easter. I went to a Baptist church once spring break. We had Bibles in the home, but I never read one of them. I believed Jesus was for real, but I am not sure I would have gone to heaven if I had died—and I almost did more than once. I've been an up close eye witness to suicide, drug overdoses and other ugly realities of the darkness of this world.

As a teenager, I got involved in alcohol and drugs of many kinds. I watched some of my friends go off the deep end with these substances in my early 20s, but managed not to follow down that road. Instead, I went to journalism school in Orlando, where I lived with my grandparents. That's where I met my ex-husband, a just-returned missionary from a false religion.

Of course, without any real understanding of the doctrines of Christ, I didn't know what his religion was all about. I just knew this ex-missionary seemed passionate about helping people. That was attractive. Thank God, I never embraced this false religion. I didn't have time to. I married the ex-missionary and soon had a baby, but he abandoned us for a young woman in a Latin American country when my daughter was just two years old. We haven't seen his face since the day he left "on assignment" for his job. That was in 1999.

I was angry with God. I remember being down on my knees at my bedside, weeping uncontrollably and screaming out through the sobs, "Why? Why? Why did you let this happen? You could have stopped this from happening!" I repeated this scene many days and many nights. I even shook my fist at God. I prayed a lot during those times and I am sure that God, in His mercy, did help me. Looking back, I can see how His plan unfolded. But the issues grew worse before they grew better.

I ended up landing in jail on a bogus charge trumped up by a dishonest female police officer. That story is a book in and of itself, and I explain more about this aspect of my testimony in my book *Fervent Faith*. Suffice it to say that I landed in the county jail at a time when a well-known evangelistic group was touring with sports stars and actors who were giving their personal testimonies about the life-changing power of Jesus. Oh, the power of a testimony! I gave my heart to the Lord and was prepared for whatever I might face—even what looked like five years in prison. Thank God that I was not convicted of those false charges. God delivered me from the mess, but it all but bankrupted me financially. I was saved, but I was still broke and hurting.

The breakthrough I live in today didn't come over night. I had to break some ungodly habits and develop the habits of victorious Christian living.

I had to come to understand my spiritual and natural gifts and begin using them. I had to become a student of the Word. I had to discover discipline, renew my mind, consecrate myself, and more. These are among the *7 Habits of Victorious Christian Living*. It wasn't easy to break the old habits and forge new ones. But it was worth it.

God has seen fit to let me travel to eight countries in three hemispheres. I've produced Christian television shows, written Christian books, built a thriving businesses in the marketplace, and, most importantly raised a daughter—as a single mother—who herself travels to the mission fields sharing the love of Jesus. I never would have made it without Jesus. But I had my part to play—I had to make a decision. And I'm going to show you how to do the same thing. God has a plan for you, and if you will adopt His habits for victorious Christian living, you can see your destiny unfold right before your eyes. It's never too late—and He'll never let you down.

CHAPTER 1

What is Victorious Christian Living?

Because a great door for effective work has opened to me, and there are many who oppose me.

—1 Corinthians 16:9 (NIV)

Before we can jump headlong into the life-changing habits of victorious Christian living, we need to understand what victorious Christian living actually is—and what is not. We need to have a clear picture of what it means to live in victory or we could pursue the wrong goals and end up in the devil's snare.

Victorious Christian living isn't necessarily sitting in TBN's studio getting interviewed by one of the Crouches. Victorious Christian living isn't necessarily teaching the Word of God to tens of thousands of people in an arena. Victorious Christian living is doing what God has called you to do—whether that's preaching the Gospel to the nations, raising your children in the admonition and fear of the Lord, conquering the marketplace, or something else—and doing it for the glory of God. Victorious Christian living is fulfilling your calling on this earth with righteousness, peace and joy in the Holy Ghost.

Jesus said, "I came that they may have and enjoy life, and have it in abundance (to the full, till it overflows)" (John 10:10 AMP). The Message translation puts it this way: "I came so they can have real and eternal life, more and better life than they ever dreamed of." Victorious Christian living promises a better life than you ever dreamed possible. It is God's unique plan for you. If He did it for me—and He did—then He'll do it for you.

Consider the promises: When you live a victorious Christian life, you won't lack any good thing. You will have an abundant life spiritually, mentally, physically, financially and socially. And you'll be a vessel God can use to help others see these promises manifest in their lives, too.

Isn't that what we all want? God sent me to tell you that all of these promises are part of your inheritance as His child. Seeing these promises manifest in your life may mean breaking some bad habits and forging some new habits. It may mean getting rid of some wrong mindsets and adopting some new mindsets. It may mean turning away from some old relationships and building some new relationships. But victorious Christian living is God's will for you. And when you determine to step into that will, the Spirit of Grace is right there to meet you—and empower you. The result of holy perseverance is fruit that remains.

Victorious Christian Living 101

We find strong examples of victorious Kingdom living—and not-so-victorious Kingdom living—throughout the Bible. Indeed, there are plenty of dos and don'ts in Scripture, from Genesis to Revelation. But let's focus for a moment on the themes we see in the Book of Acts. I focus on Acts because these believers were in the same position we are: born again, baptized with the Holy Ghost, and working out their own salvation with fear and trembling (Philippians 2:12).

One thing I notice when I study the Book of Acts is this: There seemed to be far less striving and much more relying on the Holy Spirit in the early days of the Church. There seemed to be much more boldness and willingness to stand up for the Gospel of Christ even in the face of persecution in the early days of the Church. And there seemed to be much less competition and much more unity in the early days of the Church.

Victorious Christian living begins with seeking the Kingdom of God and His righteousness—His way of being and doing right—and then you'll have everything you need and more to give to others in need (Matthew 6:33).

Remember when Peter stood up among the believers—a small group of about 120—and said they needed to choose another witness from among the men who had been with the Apostles of the Lamb during Jesus' ministry? Well, I don't read about any backbiting or campaigning going on for who would assume that position. They proposed two men, Justus and Matthias. They prayed. And they cast lots. The lot fell to Matthias (Acts 1:26).

Justus didn't pitch a fit and leave the church when Matthias was chosen. He didn't get bitter. He didn't tell his friend why he was the better choice and question the discernment of the leadership. I believe Justus waited in the Upper Room with the rest of the 120 for the promise of the Holy Spirit so he could get busy being a witness. I believe Justus was more concerned with pleasing God than looking like a big shot in front of men. And I believe Justus lived a victorious Christian life and fulfilled his destiny.

I challenge you to re-read the Book of Acts. If we prayed like that, loved like that, walked like that, talked like that—if we lived like that—then we would see greater manifestations of Christ's power in our lives and ministries. We would be more peaceful, more prosperous, and more effective for the Kingdom. We would live more victorious Christian lives. The good news is we can commit to that right now. The bad news is there will be opposition. But even that's not bad news because God always leads us into triumph in Christ (2 Corinthians 2:14). We just have to make up our minds to live like who we are— children of the King. His grace is sufficient.

Opposition to Christian Living

Can I be bold? Victorious Christian living means more than adopting a different way of life than the world. It also means adopting a different way of life than mainstream born-again believers. No one said it would be easy. We may not be living in tents like the believers of the early Church did. But we face other challenges in the 21st Century that the early Christians couldn't even conceive.

The Apostle Paul understood that believers in his time and in the ages to come would have to engage in wrestling matches with principalities and powers. That's why he wrote passages about putting on the whole armor of God (Ephesians 6). And that's why he imparted to his spiritual son Timothy the seven habits of victorious Christian living that we'll explore in this book.

Paul knew that keeping the Gospel alive in a world where the devil roams about like a roaring lion would demand faithfulness, diligence, focus, holiness, and more. The good news is we can live a victorious Christian life instead of a lukewarm, ineffective, boring religious life—if we follow the Apostle Paul's time-tested advice.

As you read about the seven habits in the following chapters, remember that prayer is a major part of change. Apart from Him, we can do nothing (John 15:15). Developing the habits of victorious Christian living means leaning on God to help us manifest the divine nature of which we are partakers (2 Peter 1:4).

Don't strive. This book is not some step-by-step formula that will produce magical results—and it's not a prescription for works of the flesh, either. Just get into agreement with His will and yield to His Spirit. And be encouraged. The Apostle Paul's Holy Spirit-inspired letter to the church at Philippi assures us we can do all things through Christ who strengthens us (Philippians 4:13).

Breakthrough Exercise: Accept Responsibility

Are you ready to embark on the journey to discovering and adopting the seven habits of victorious Christian living that lead to breakthrough? Before you move on to the next chapter, take a moment to complete this action exercise:

As you make your way through this book, the devil will whisper all manner of excuses for not adopting these biblical habits. The enemy will help you find a laundry list of people to blame for why you can't live a victorious Christian life. I can tell you from experience that you won't find victory in blaming your parents, your spouse, your siblings, your kids, your boss—or anyone else. Blame is a guard to change. So don't even blame yourself. Just accept responsibility for where you are right now—and accept responsibility for changing where you are right now. God will meet you there.

Remember this: You are responsible. Theodore Roosevelt, the 26th president of the United States, once said, "If you could kick the person in the pants responsible for most of your trouble, you wouldn't sit down for a month." (Hint, hint… he's talking about you.)

Nothing changes in your life until you take responsibility. No, you can't help what people did or do to you. But you can take responsibility for how you respond. You can decide to be a victim or a victor. So determine now to be responsible for exercising the seven habits of victorious

Christian living. You're the only one who can. I assure you, victory lies just ahead.

Are you ready to accept responsibility? Take a moment right now to consider the areas of your life that need adjusting, repent for any sins you've committed, receive God's forgiveness and grace, and set your mind to change your life. Let's go!

CHAPTER 2

Victory Habit #1
Stir Up the Gift

The special gift of ministry you received when I laid hands on you and prayed—keep that ablaze! God doesn't want us to be shy with His gifts, but bold and loving and sensible.

—2 Timothy 1:6-7 (The Message)

Have you stirred up your gift lately? The Apostle Paul told Timotheus to stir up the gift of God—and keep it stirred up. I like how the Amplified Bible puts it: "Stir up (rekindle the embers of, fan the flame of, and keep burning) the [gracious] gift of God, [the inner fire] that is in you…" (2 Timothy 1:6 AMP).

We know that Paul was talking about the gift of the Holy Ghost in this Scripture—and it's vital to build yourself up in your most holy faith by praying in the Spirit (Jude 1:20)—but victorious Christian living also means exercising your natural God-given gifts and talents. If you can build a wall, get some bricks and mortar and start building. If you can drive a van, pick up people and take them church. It's not all about preaching, praying and prophesying. Jesus also expects you to use your God-given gifts and talents to advance the Kingdom.

Some people have many talents; others have only one. But everybody has at least one. The Lord may let you sit for a season or two so you can receive healing from the world's (or the Church's) wounds and get equipped for battle. But there comes a time when you'll be called on to use your gift.

I don't believe we are completely fulfilled if we aren't doing what God called us to do. American Philosopher and Educational Reformer John Dewey said this: "To find out what one is fitted to do, and to secure an opportunity to do it, is the key to happiness." I see the truth in that. Victorious Christian living doesn't make a career out of warming the pew—or even dancing in the Spirit with Charismatic flare on Sunday mornings. Victorious Christian living demands more from us. We need to be sensitive to the Holy Spirit to invest our time, talents and money where He leads us to invest them.

Investing Your Gifts in the Kingdom

The concept of using your God-given talents to bring Kingdom increase is biblical, isn't it? Remember the Parable of the Talents? In Matthew 25, Jesus told the story of a man who was about to go on a long journey. He called his servants together and entrusted his possessions to them. To one he gave five talents, to another he gave two talents, and to another he gave one talent.

The distribution of talents was according to each man's ability. In other words, the master knew how much the servants could handle and he wasn't expecting them to do more than what they were capable of doing. If he expected more than that, he would have been deemed unjust.

God is the same way with us. He knows what gifts, talents and abilities He's given us—better than we do. God isn't expecting more from us than He's made us capable of. That would be unjust and God is not unjust in any wise. He gave us talents for a reason—to use for His glory. Our just God is expecting us to faithfully use the gifts and talents He created us with. Like money and possessions, He expects us to be good stewards of our natural and spiritual gifts. When we are, He'll pick up where our abilities leave off to accomplish the supernatural.

Let's get back to the Parable of the Talents. You know the story. The man with five talents immediately began trading with them and gained five more talents. The man who had received two talents also doubled his money. But the man who had received one talent went away, dug a hole in the ground, and hid his master's money because he was afraid. When the master returned, he commended the servants who had increased their investments. He called the other servant a wicked, lazy slave and gave his talent to the man with 10 talents (Matthew 25:26-28).

Facing Down Fear

The man with one talent used fear as an excuse. If you are going to use your God-given gifts and talents for His glory, for His purposes, for His Kingdom, then you are going to have to face down fear—more than once. In his wisdom and experience, Paul knew this. So right after he exhorted Timothy to "stir up the gift," he gave him the skinny on how to combat the spirit of fear that would undoubtedly come to try to stop him. Paul reminded Timothy that fear does not emanate from the Spirit of God (2 Timothy 1:7). Armed with an understanding of fear's source, Timothy was better equipped to resist this Gospel opposition when it reared its ugly head. Paul encouraged Timothy to walk in the power of the Holy Ghost, the love of God, and the sound mind of Christ rather than cringing and fawning in the face of fear.

Again, the wicked servant in the Parable of the Talents was too scared to use his gift, so he rendered his gift useless by hiding it from the world. When God gives you a gift, He expects you to use it—and use it with confidence and boldness as you rely on the Gift Giver to back you up. Let's listen in to the confrontation:

> "The servant given one thousand said, 'Master, I know you have high standards and hate careless ways, that you demand the best and make no allowances for error. I was afraid I might disappoint you, so I found a good hiding place and secured your money. Here it is, safe and sound down to the last cent.' The master was furious. 'That's a terrible way to live! It's criminal to live cautiously like that! If you knew I was after the best, why did you do less than the least? The least you could have done would have been to invest the sum with the bankers, where at least I would have gotten a little interest. Take the thousand and give it to the one who risked the most. And get rid of this 'play-it-safe' who won't go out on a limb. Throw him out into utter darkness."

—Matthew 25:24-30 (The Message)

That should get our attention. This wicked, lazy servant understood enough about the ways of his master to know he was a man of excellence who demanded the best. Instead of diligently looking for the best opportunities to invest his talent—keep in mind that he could merely have mirrored the investments of the other two servants—he let fear of failing and a slack hand lead him into a decision that destroyed his destiny. If he had been bold and diligent like his contemporaries, he would have been deemed a good and faithful servant and assigned "ruler over many things" even though he started out with much less talent than his counterparts. But instead of receiving a promotion and entering into the joy of the Lord, he was cast into utter darkness.

I'm not saying that the Lord is going to cast you into utter darkness if you don't use your God-given gifts to bring increase to the Kingdom. You are saved by faith, not by works. Of course, faith without works is dead, isn't it? (James 2:20). Faith without works doesn't breed victorious Christian living. Paul knew enough about the ways of his Master to know He doesn't like timidity. God likes boldness that comes from faith. Paul was as bold as they come and he wanted to make sure Timothy didn't shrink back in fear on the Gospel battlefield.

Benjamin Franklin once said, "Hide not your talents, they for use were made. What's a sundial in the shade?" In other words, if you take the sundial out of the sun it can't fulfill its purpose. A sundial only can only serve its purpose—to tell time—when it stays in the sun. Likewise, we can only serve our purpose when we stay in the Son. Victorious Christian living means walking in the Son, not hiding our talents in fear's shade. Our talents for God's use were made. Amen?

Let me put it another way. God has given each and every one of us talents. When we stand before Him one day, He is not going to want to hear, "I was too scared to invest my talent in the Kingdom because I didn't want the persecution." He'll still love you, and He'll forgive you. But actions produced by fear don't please Him—only actions produced by faith cut muster with the King. Eighteenth Century British Writer and Clergyman Sydney Smith once said, "A great deal of talent is lost to the world of the want of a little courage."

I've had to face down fear plenty of times—and will have to face down fear plenty more times. As one who has a recognizable name in secular media—and as one who has a recognizable name in Christian media—I used to fear the lines crossing. I feared that my secular clients would drop me like a hot potato if they realized that I was a prophetic voice in the Church and wrote about polarizing issues—and took God's side (which is usually the opposite of theirs).

My fear manifested this way: I had two separate identities. I felt like Clark Kent, who worked for a newspaper until an emergency arose and then he became a superhero. Not that I consider myself a super Christian, but you get the point. I was living a dual life because I was afraid that if the world found out my role in the church they'd force kryptonite down my throat and kill my business. After all, much of the secular media is about as liberal as it gets. It took me some years to get over that. But through the habits I share in this book, I faced down that fear and God was able to promote me in Christian media for His glory and still prosper me by means of the secular marketplace. I've even run into a few Christians along the secular media way who support me.

Victorious Christian living requires us to fan the flame of passion and boldness within us because there will be those who seek to drench our revolutionary dreams with rivers of negativity, apathy and even religious opposition. If God has called you to do something seemingly impossible with your gift, take on the attitude of Walt Disney, "It's kind of fun to do the impossible," and then remember nothing is impossible with God (Luke 1:37). It's not you who is doing it anyway. It's Him working through you.

Schooling the Gift

If anyone had a gift, it was the classical composer Ludwig van Beethoven. We're still benefiting from his gift today. I like what the German composer said, "Then let us all do what is right, strive with all our might toward the unattainable, develop as fully as we can the gifts God has given us, and never stop learning."

I like this because it's not enough to use the gifts, we also need to school the gifts. In other words, we need to continue to feed our gifts. In that way, we stir them up, keep them sharp and fresh, and make them ready for the Master's use.

God has given me the opportunity to use my gifts in many ways. I remember when I first got saved. I was a journalist and editor in the marketplace. I didn't know exactly what God had called me to do, but I clearly recognized that God had given me a gift to communicate in various forms. (When I was in kindergarten, my schoolteacher told my mother I would be a writer one day. She didn't know she was prophesying over my life.) Of course, I plugged into a church and started serving in whatever capacity I could. I vacuumed floors. I licked envelopes. I worked in the nursery (not at all my grace!). I handled the book and tape table at conferences. Soon, I began editing letters for the pastor.

I was glad to be used of God in any way; thrilled to serve the Master. Of course, I knew that most of what I was doing wasn't in line with my gifts and talents. So I started writing to Christian magazines with story ideas, figuring this was one way to exercise my talent for the Kingdom. My zeal was there but my timing was off. Truth is, I didn't know enough of God's Word to write for a Christian magazine when I first got saved. I had to school myself, so to speak, in the Word and ways of God and get some experience under my belt so I had something to say; something that would help somebody.

Soon enough, my pursuit of service to God began to bear fruit. I'll never forget the day I was driving home from an assignment with a major newswire. An SUV had rolled over and killed an entire family. I had to interview surviving family members after a news conference that divulged the cause of the accident as faulty tires. As I was waiting in the press room, listening to the hardened hearts of journalists making vulgar jokes about last weekend's party, my spirit was grieved. I reported on the tragedy and drove home prayerfully. That's when the Lord spoke to my heart, "I've given you gifts. I expect you to use them."

I knew what He meant. God was drawing me to use the gifts and talents He had given me for His glory, and not merely as a means of paying my bills. I continued working with this newswire, and within a few weeks the Lord spoke to me a second time while I was on assignment. He told me something amazing that you probably wouldn't believe if I wrote it. Suffice it to say that it more than confirmed my call into ministry, but it was some time before others recognized it. I had to enter the School of the Holy Ghost.

Maybe you do, too. Or maybe you need a university degree to school the gift in you. Maybe you need practical experience in a specific field through internships. Or maybe you just need to read every book you can find on the subject of your gift and exercise what you learn.

The point is this: No matter whether your gift is writing, preaching, architecting, retailing, doctoring, or something else, God has given you that gift and He expects you to use it for His glory. In order to bring increase to the Master, we need to identify and school our gift so we can be among the best in whatever field God has called us to.

Nineteenth Century Swiss Philosopher and Poet Henri Frederic Amiel put it this way: "Work while you have light. You are responsible for the talent that has been entrusted to you." Can somebody say amen?

Breakthrough Exercise: Identify Your Gift

Are you ready to stir up your gift? Not even sure what it is? It can be frustrating to want to serve God with your whole heart and not know what your God-given gift is. Don't let frustration get the best of you. The steps below will help you identify your gift and get your breakthrough.

1. Pray in the Spirit. If you are born again and filled with the Holy Spirit, you can stir up the Spirit of God within you. The Holy Spirit is your Teacher. He's the Spirit of revelation. He'll show you what your gift is. You have to press in, pursue, and not give up. Jesus promised you will find if you just keep seeking. God is not trying to hide your purpose or your gifts from you.

2. Ask people you know. If you aren't sure what your God-given gifts and talents are, ask your family, friends, and brothers and sisters in Christ. Sometimes other see what you can't. Then pray some more.

3. What are you naturally good at? Usually our gifts are related to things we are naturally good at. But sometimes you have to drill down into how to apply what you are good at to Kingdom work. Some are natural conversationalists. That might not help you earn a living, but it can help you make people feel welcome at church and reach out to people with the love of God.

4. What's your passion? Your gift is often related to your passion. But again, sometimes you have to dig a little deeper to determine how that passion for sports, dancing or filmmaking relates to a gift that can bring increase into the Kingdom.

5. Step out in faith. If you really have no idea what your gift is, then try different activities in your local church. Go on an outreach. Work in the nursery. Volunteer in the bookstore. Sometimes our gifts become apparent in the midst of serving.

CHAPTER 3

Victory Habit #2
Know the Word

Study to shew thyself approved unto God, a workman that needeth not to be ashamed, rightly dividing the word of truth.

—2 Timothy 2:15

Know the Word. And again I say, know the Word. Especially in this day and age, when there is so much deception making its way through the Body of Christ, we need to know the Word—and the Word needs to be the final judge in every matter. After all, it's the truth in God's Word that we understand and walk in by the power of the Holy Spirit that makes (and keeps) us free (John 8:32).

Paul understood this all too well. He dealt head on with First Century heresies working to seep into the Church. He knew that the only way to combat deceiving doctrines was with the Sword of the Spirit, which is the Word of God. Paul charged Timothy to know the Word of God; to study it so he could teach it to others accurately. Let's listen to the apostle's direct advice once again:

> "Study and be eager to present yourself to God approved (tested by trial), a workman who has no cause to be ashamed, correctly analyzing and accurately dividing [rightly handling and skillfully teaching] the Word of Truth."
>
> —2 Timothy 2:15 (AMP)

Think about it for a minute. Paul isn't telling Timothy to breeze through the Word for 15 minutes a day—or even to read the Word for an hour a day. Paul is calling Timothy to a deeper acquaintance with the Truth. Paul is telling Timothy to analyze the Word. Merriam-Webster defines *analyze* as "to study or determine the nature and relationship of the parts of by analysis." Paul was calling Timothy to study the Word in a way that took into account the whole counsel of God so he could see how everything fit together, line upon line, precept upon precept. Paul didn't want Timothy to take a Scripture out of context and use it to build some doctrine or establish some mindset that would introduce error into his ministry. Paul also didn't want Timothy to be ignorant of the doctrines of Christ because ignorance opens the door to heresy. Paul wanted his spiritual son to analyze the Word—and correctly analyze it. That's a different approach than just reading the Word, and one that guards against error.

Paul also told Timothy to accurately divide the Word. The Darby translation says, "cutting in a straight line the Word of Truth." Paul stressed to Timothy the importance of properly handling and skillfully teaching God's Word. In Paul's day, just as in modern times, there were many false teachers mishandling the Word of God and convincingly teaching error. Paul knew Timothy would have to come against some of the same heresies he himself worked to combat. It was vital then, and it's vital now, to study the Word. Indeed, victorious Christian living demands devotion to truly comprehending—and sharing—the Word of God.

Power in God's Word

There is power in God's Word. The Bible calls the Word the Sword of the Spirit. Merriam-Webster defines a sword as "a weapon with a long blade for cutting or thrusting that is often used as a symbol of honor or authority."

God's Word is not "like" a weapon. God's Word "is" a weapon. We can put it in our mouths, just like Jesus did, and cut the enemy's plans to shreds, just like Jesus did. Jesus demonstrated how to wield the Sword of the Spirit during His 40-day wilderness experience. No matter what doubtful deliberations, jilted justifications, or twisted truths Satan introduced to His mind, Jesus just told the devil what the Word of God said. You might say Jesus schooled the Devil on the uncompromising truth. When Satan tried to distort God's commands or take them out of context, Jesus was able to correctly analyze and rightly divide the Word of Truth.

Jesus could not be deceived by the lies of the enemy. The bad news is, unlike Jesus, we are capable of being deceived. The good news is we can guard our hearts and minds in Christ Jesus by becoming students of the Word and praying God's Word in faith. By keeping the Word at the forefront of our minds, we can more quickly discern teachings and situations that don't agree with the Spirit of the Word. On the flip side, by keeping the Word at the forefront of our minds, we can more readily receive all of God's promises, which are yes and amen. By studying the Word to show ourselves approved, we are approving ourselves for His blessings. In other words, we are sowing seed in our hearts that will yield Kingdom fruit. We are making ourselves ready to receive all of what Jesus died to give us.

Aren't you glad that God is changing you from glory to glory (2 Corinthians 3:18)? Victorious Christian living yields to the Holy Spirit's work in us—and yields to the truth revealed in the Word. It's a one-two combination that squeezes the devil out of our mindsets, bit by bit, until our minds are renewed. It's an exchange that continues as Jesus moves to complete the good work He started in us (Philippians 1:6).

Cooperating with the Word

Of course, we have a part to play in our sanctification, and the Word has a part to play in our sanctification. You can see your part and the Word's part in this Scripture:

> "So get rid of all uncleanness and the rampant outgrowth of wickedness, and in a humble (gentle, modest) spirit receive and welcome the Word which implanted and rooted [in your hearts] contains the power to save your souls."

> —James 1: 21 (AMP)

Our part is to humbly receive the Word of God and make a solid decision to rid our lives of anything that doesn't agree with it. Victorious Christians understand that this isn't a one-time exercise. The Word needs to get rooted in our hearts before it can bear fruit, and that requires studying and meditating Scripture every day. If we do our part, the Word will do its part. The Word of God never fails, and meditating on the Word is one of the best time investments you can make.

So what is the Word's part? When we humbly receive God's Word, it unleashes power in our lives. This power renews our minds so that we can see the world from God's perspective and ultimately live in visible victory. Where we were conditioned by our past to expect lack, the mind renewed with God's Word expects—and therefore believes for and receives—prosperity. Where we were conditioned by our heredity to expect sickness, the mind renewed with God's Word expects—and therefore believes and receives—divine health. I could go on and on. The bottom line is that the mind renewed with God's Word expects—and therefore believes and receives—everything God promises.

We need to love the Word of God with all our heart, all our soul, all our strength and all our mind (Luke 10:27). That shouldn't be a struggle considering how sweet it is—but sometimes pride gets in the way. We think we can do something apart from Jesus so we run out into the world ill-equipped and we fail. Remember, we are supposed to receive the Word with humility. Truly, there is no other way to receive it. If we have a haughty spirit, we need to renounce it, repent, receive forgiveness, and welcome the Word with meekness.

We need to meditate on the Word of God in the area of our weakness. Maybe it's not pride. Maybe it's anger. Maybe it's gossiping. Maybe it's jealousy. Whatever your weakness, there is power in God's Word to help your soul prosper against it—for His glory! Consider the Word of the Lord that came to Isaiah:

> "So shall My word be that goes forth out of My mouth: it shall not return to Me void [without producing any effect, useless], but it shall accomplish that which I please and purpose, and it shall prosper in the thing for which I sent it."

—Isaiah 55: 11 (AMP)

Unleashing God's Power

You can speak the Word of God over your own life—and that's what victorious Christian people do. If you are struggling in an area, if you need a specific promise of God to manifest in your life, then speak the Word in faith. Renew your mind to the Word that offers the provision for your need. Ask God to manifest in your life what the Word says belongs to you. Have confidence that if you ask anything according to His will, He hears you—and God's Word is His will (1 John 5:14). Be bold. Be assured that if you ask, it will be given to you (Matthew 7:7). And ask in the name of Jesus. Jesus said, "You may ask me for anything in my name, and I will do it" (John 14:14). What a promise! Never doubt it!

You should also make a confession list. There is power in the Word of God that you confess over your life. I have a confession list that's about 15 pages. One list deals with who I am in Christ. The other deals with Scriptural promises I'd like to see manifest; things I am believing for. I can honestly tell you that in just a few short years of confessing the Word over my life, I ended up with major victories, including healing from high blood pressure. I am also debt-free and own two properties. I am doing what I am called to do, and I have much more peace in my life than I once thought possible. Confessing the Word of God over your life brings results. Stick with it. Victorious Christian living relies on the power in God's Word, not in the power of self. And God's Word is powerful. Consider the Spirit-inspired words from the writer of Hebrews:

"For the Word that God speaks is alive and full of power [making it active, operative, energizing, and effective]; it is sharper than any two-edged sword, penetrating to the dividing line of the breath of life (soul) and [the immortal] spirit, and of joints and marrow [of the deepest parts of our nature], exposing and sifting and analyzing and judging the very thoughts and purposes of the heart."

—Hebrews 4:12 (AMP)

I find it interesting that Paul tells Timothy to analyze the Word of God—because the Word of God analyzes us. To me, this signifies a symbiotic relationship between the people of God and the Word of God. Symbiotic means "the living together in more or less intimate association." Victorious Christian living requires an intimate association with the Word. We need to analyze the Word and extract the truth we need for our daily lives, moment to moment. The Word analyzes us and shows us, like a mirror, where we need to yield to the grace of God as we become more like Jesus. There's no striving. No struggling. No frustration. Just an intimate relationship with a loving God whose thoughts are higher than our thoughts and whose ways are higher than our ways (Isaiah 55:9) Thank God, He has given us His thoughts and made record of His ways in His Word. It shouldn't be a challenge to delight ourselves in it.

Delight Yourself in the Word

As I write this, I am delighting myself in the Word. When I read the Word, or in this case write about the Word, I am filled with joy because I can see the inherent power in it to change me, to empower me, to comfort me…God has given us everything we need for life and godliness (2 Peter 1:3). He has given us His Word and His Spirit and blessed us with every spiritual blessing in the heavenly places in Christ (Ephesians 1:3). In the Word of God we find out what belongs to us and what our rightful inheritance is in Christ—and it's delightful! David said, "I will delight myself in your statutes; I will not forget your word" (Psalm 119:16). We need to do as David did: meditate on His precepts and have respect for His ways (119:15). We need to delight in the law of the Lord (Psalm 1:2). His testimonies should be our delight and our counselor (Psalm 119:24). Let us never forget that the one who fears the Lord and delights greatly in His commandments is blessed (Psalm 112:1).

As you can see, delighting in the Word of God is a continual theme throughout the Book of Psalms. But what does it mean to delight yourself in the Word? Do you really know? Delighting is not complicated, but it's important to understand just what the Word of God is telling us to do so that we can do it indeed. Simply stated, to delight in something is to take great pleasure in it. When you are delighted, you are highly pleased. You have joy and satisfaction. The Word of God should be a source of joy. It should satisfy the soul. It should delight you—and it will if you truly know the Word.

Embracing Prophetic Ministry

Up until now, we've been talking about the written Word of God—the Scriptures found in the 66 books of the Bible. But what about prophetic words? What advice did Paul give to Timothy, and his other spiritual children, about prophecy? Plenty.

Under the inspiration of the Holy Spirit, Paul said things like this: "We know in part, and we prophesy in part" (1 Corinthians 13:9). Only God knows everything, and we only know what He decides to reveal to us. He has given us the Scriptures, which we can stake our lives on. I believe in and exercise prophetic ministry. But we have to remember that even accurate prophecy doesn't always give us all the answers. We see through a glass darkly (1 Corinthians 13:12). Victorious Christian living doesn't put prophecy above, or even on the same par, with Scripture.

"Despise not prophesyings. Prove all things; hold fast that which is good" (1 Thessalonians 5:20). Unfortunately, some quench the Spirit of God's voice by shunning prophecy. We should embrace prophetic ministry because it's vital. But victorious Christians do not believe every spirit. We try the spirits to see if they are of God (1 John 4:1). In other words, victorious Christians value prophetic ministry but judge prophetic words.

"Neglect not the gift that is in thee, which was given thee by prophecy, with the laying on of the hands of the presbytery (1 Timothy 4:13-15). Victorious Christian living takes into account prophetic words that have been judged as accurate, meditates on them, and takes action on the truth within them.

"This charge I commit unto thee, son Timothy, according to the prophecies which went before on thee, that thou by them mightest war a good warfare; Holding faith, and a good conscience; which some having put away concerning faith have made shipwreck" (1 Timothy 17-19). Victorious Christian living speaks out prophetic words to battle any opposition to God's revealed plan for your individual life.

Remember this, the Word and the Spirit agree. It's great to get a prophetic word, but let's make sure that everything we do agrees with the spirit of the written Word of God. Again, I believe in prophetic ministry—I've been called to function in that gift. But I'll be the first one to admit that questionable personal prophecy has led to instability in some believers who don't understand how to judge prophetic utterances. (For more on judging prophetic words, check out my book "27 Ways to Judge Prophecy.")

Always remember this:

> "Every Scripture is God-breathed (given by His inspiration) and profitable for instruction, for reproof and conviction of sin, for correction of error and discipline in obedience, [and] for training in righteousness (in holy living, in conformity to God's will in thought, purpose, and action)."
>
> —2 Timothy 3: 16 (AMP)

Not every prophetic word is God-breathed, or given by His inspiration. There are three sources of prophecy: God's spirit, the human spirit, or an evil spirit. There is profit in God's unadulterated Word, whether it's Scripture or prophecy. But when the word is abused—whether Scripture or prophecy—there is the danger of it leading people away from Christ instead of to Christ. This is the mark of deception.

A Word About Deception

In order to walk in the fullness of the abundant life Jesus died to give us, and in order to guard ourselves from deception, we need to know the Word. Jesus Himself warned us to take heed that we not be deceived (Luke 21:8). Paul was well acquainted with the deception seeping into the Body of Christ in his day. And he knew that if ministers of the Gospel didn't work to understand and teach the unadulterated Word of God to others it would ultimately endanger the Church.

God is coming back for a glorious church without spot or wrinkle or any such thing; one that is holy and without blemish (Ephesians 5:27). Deception is certainly a blemish. Listen saint, we are all responsible for studying the Word for ourselves. Even if a trusted minister is bringing the Word, you still need to study it out for yourself.

Paul told the church in Corinth, "Be not deceived" (1 Corinthians 6:9; 1 Corinthians 15:33). Paul also told the church in Galatia, "Be not deceived" (Galatians 6:7). Paul told the church at Ephesus, "Let no man deceive you with vain words: for because of these things cometh the wrath of God upon the children of disobedience" (Ephesians 5:6). Paul told the church at Thessalonica, "Let no man deceive you by any means: for that day shall not come, except there come a falling away first, and that man of sin be revealed, the son of perdition" (2

Thessalonians 2:3). And Paul told Timothy, "Evil men and seducers shall wax worse and worse, deceiving, and being deceived" (2 Timothy 3:13).

Why would Paul need to tell born-again believers not to be deceived? Because its possible for a born-again believe to be deceived. Other apostles also warned against deception. It's a running theme throughout both the Old Testament and New Testament, actually. John warned not to let any man deceive you (1 John 3:7) and that many deceivers have entered into the world (2 John 1:7).

Jesus warned, "For there shall arise false Christs, and false prophets, and shall shew great signs and wonders; insomuch that, if it were possible, they shall deceive the very elect" (Matthew 24:5). Jesus also said, "Take heed that no man deceive you" (Matthew 24:4). He said, "Many false prophets shall rise, and shall deceive many" (Matthew 24:11). Unfortunately, I've sat in churches where major deception lived. The first church I ever attended turned out to be led by a false prophet. Even as a brand new born-again believer, I knew something was wrong—and I got out of there fast.

Some years later, I was in a church that started off on the right foot—offering God-breathed revelation that strengthened many—but ended up in a deceptive ditch by essentially exalting the demonic spirits with excessive spiritual warfare teaching instead of exalting Christ. Leaving that church was much harder because of all the soul ties I had formed over the many years I spent there. But if I hadn't left I would have ended up deceived like the rest of them, and forfeiting much of the victory I walk in by the grace of God. Study the Word for yourself. Every preacher makes mistakes, but if you are in a church where the pastor is twisting Scripture and adding strange interpretations to it, or using the Word to control or merchandise people, get out before you come under that same spirit of error. I assure you, beloved, there's no victory there.

Prophetic Deception

Some years ago I went to a conference in the northeast United States. There was one particular minister of whom I was especially fond. I had many of this person's CDs and they had inspired me to come up higher in areas such as prayer. I listened intently to the opening message at the conference. The anointing was strong. I was shouting with the rest of the believers as the Word of God brought life into the room.

Then it happened. Something unexpected that left my stomach in a knot. This minister, who had just preached the unadulterated Word of God with a strong anointing, stepped out into a manipulative realm of presumption and merchandising. This minister prophesied that whomever would sow $1,000 into the ministry would receive a powerful prayer mantle—right then and there. In fact, as a symbol of that spiritual prayer mantle, this minister was going to give each sower a special prayer shawl before imparting this "supernatural ability" to them. I stood and watched for just long enough to make sure my eyes and ears weren't playing tricks on me. The minister cried, "Hurry, hurry, come up here fast with your money!" I moved fast alright. I went out a side door, through the back halls of the hotel, and out into the streets of the city. I was sickened by what I saw being done in the name of Jesus.

I doubt anyone at the conference ever saw it coming. The message was pure, but the merchandising tactics afterwards wreaked to high heaven. So I asked the Lord what was going on. I asked Him why there was such a strong anointing on this minister's preaching (before the altar call). His answer was simple: "There is an anointing on My Word." And this is true. So long as the pure Word was being preached, the Holy Spirit was there to confirm it. But I tell you the truth, when this minister started twisting the Word of God for money, the anointing lifted off that meeting faster than green grass through a goose. The only thing left was hype, hype and more hype as unsuspecting believers looking for a supernatural breakthrough in their prayer life lined up with credit cards to charge their way to prosperity.

The True Five-Fold

This is a travesty. The true five-fold has been given to the Church to help believers avoid the snares of deception. And too many times five-fold ministers gone bad are the ones leading the sheep right off the edge of the deceptive cliff. Let's look at the purpose of the five-fold:

> "And he gave some, apostles; and some, prophets; and some, evangelists; and some, pastors and teachers; For the perfecting of the saints, for the work of the ministry, for the edifying of the body of Christ: Till we all come in the unity of the faith, and of the knowledge of the Son of God, unto a perfect man, unto the measure of the stature of the fulness of Christ:
>
> That we henceforth be no more children, tossed to and fro, and carried about with every wind of doctrine, by the sleight of men, and cunning craftiness, whereby they lie in wait to deceive; But speaking the truth in love, may grow up into him in all things, which is the head, even Christ."

> —Ephesians 4:11-15

True apostles, prophets, evangelists, pastors and teachers will work to guard the sheep from deceitful doctrines that seek to control them, fleece them, and otherwise spiritually abuse them. Unfortunately, some who call themselves five-fold ministers are propagating deception to line their pockets with greenbacks. Check out my book, "The Heart of the Prophetic" to understand the true call and character of the prophet.

Yes, where the Spirit of the Lord is, there is liberty. I submit to you that the Spirit of the Lord is found where the truth of the Word is being preached. True liberty is living in the pure Word of God, not living in a distorted doctrine that seeks to elevate some spiritual gifts over others, control the sheep, fleece the flock, or abuse the elders.

Even if you are plugged into a local church headed by a minister who has strayed from the truth, it's still your responsibility to work out your own salvation with fear and trembling (Philippians 2:13). When you stand before God on Judgment Day, He's not going to give you a pass because your pastor didn't rightly divide the Word of truth. He's given you His Word so that you can rightly divide the Word of truth for yourself. Don't continue to sit under teaching that you know isn't true.

I believe the Holy Spirit tries to warn us when we are sitting under deceptive teaching. Victorious Christian leaving means studying the Word and understanding the ways of God. In doing so, we guard our hearts from the seeds of deception the devil plants so we won't reap a harvest of destruction in our spiritual lives.

The Ploy of Self-Deception

But let's get real. It doesn't take a false prophet or a false Christ to deceive you. You can do a fine job of deceiving yourself. The Apostle Paul warned of it, saying that if a man thinks himself to be something, when he is nothing, he deceives himself (Galatians 6:3). The Amplified Bible makes it a little plainer: "For if any person thinks himself to be somebody [too important to condescend to shoulder another's load] when he is nobody [of superiority except in his own estimation], he deceives and deludes and cheats himself."

Again, in 1 Corinthians 3:17 (AMP), Paul warns about self-deception: "Let no person deceive himself. If anyone among you supposes that he is wise in this age, let him become a fool [let him discard his worldly discernment and recognize himself as dull, stupid, and foolish, without true learning and scholarship], that he may become [really] wise."

Thank God, James gives us the antidote to deception: "Be doers of the Word [obey the message], and not merely listeners to it, betraying yourselves [into deception by reasoning contrary to the Truth]" (James 1:22 AMP). This is victorious Christian living.

Beloved, hear me as I recite the words of the Apostle Paul to his dear son Timothy: "Evil men and seducers shall wax worse and worse, deceiving and being deceived" (2 Timothy 3:13). I beseech you by the mercies of God not to allow yourself to be deceived and not to deceive others. If you have done either, repent now and receive forgiveness, and then get back on the narrow way. Remember, the Word of the Lord is lamp to your feet and a light to your path (Psalm 119:105). Lay up the Word in your heart that you might not sin against the Lord (Psalm 119:1).

Breakthrough Exercise: Tithe Your Time

Victorious Christian living is living in the Word. Only a firm foundation laid by God's Word stands in the midst of shakings. Of course, you can't sit and study the Word of God 24/7/365—and you wouldn't make much of an impact in the world if all you did was study and pray. So what's the answer?

I learned something from Gloria Copeland, who learned it from Kenneth E. Hagin, which I have found helpful—Give God a tithe of your time. Here is a prophecy Hagin delivered in 1982:

> "Don't take up all your time with natural things. Some of those things are legitimate and it's alright to take a certain period of time there, but see to it that you give heed unto your spirit. Give your spirit opportunity to feed upon the Word of God, and give your spirit opportunity to commune with the Father above. Build yourself up on your most holy faith by praying in the Spirit. It doesn't take a lot of time, just an hour or two out of 24. Just pay a tithe of your time unto me, saith the Lord, and all will be well with you. Your life will be changed. It will be empowered and you will be a mighty force for God."

If you don't see any way to give God an hour of your time right now, just give Him what you can. God is a multiplier. He will multiply what you give Him and supernaturally make it possible for you to spend more time with Him and in His Word—if that's the desire of your heart.

CHAPTER 4

Victory Habit #3
Hold Tightly to the Truth

If ye continue in My Word, then are ye My disciples indeed; And ye shall know the truth, and the truth shall make you free.

—John 8:31-32

Paul poured himself into Timothy. Like a good spiritual father, Paul taught Timothy the doctrines of Christ, modeled the way, and kept him in prayer. Paul also had expectations of his spiritual son. Paul expected Timothy to hold on to the sound teaching he had received; to hold tightly to the truth that is in Christ Jesus. This goes a step beyond just knowing the Word. There are plenty who have known the Word since they were tots but didn't hold tightly to it. They ended up backsliding into the devil's plan for their lives.

Paul's exact words were: "Hold fast the form of sound words, which thou hast heard of me, in faith and love which is in Christ Jesus. That good thing which was committed unto thee keep by the Holy Ghost which dwelleth in us" (2 Timothy 1:13-14).

The Amplified Bible draws it out with a little more exhortation: "Hold fast and follow the pattern of wholesome and sound teaching which you have heard from me, in [all] the faith and love which are [for us] in Christ Jesus. Guard and keep [with the greatest care] the precious and excellently adapted [Truth] which has been entrusted [to you], by the [help of the] Holy Spirit who makes His home in us" (2 Timothy 1:13 AMP).

This is the same Paul that encouraged the Corinthians to rejoice in the truth (1 Corinthians 13:6). The same Paul that stood up against the Apostle Peter because he "walked not uprightly according to the truth" when the Jews visited Antioch (Galatians 2:14). Even Paul's boasting was found in truth (2 Corinthians 7:4). Paul knew that truth was part of his spiritual armor (Ephesians 6:14) and he wasn't about to let the devil get one up on him by straying from the truth.

Nothing was more important to the Paul than

truth (2 Corinthians 11:10). He worked to impart this value to his spiritual son. Why? Because, ultimately, it's the truth that not only sets us free but also keeps us free. Where we are walking in anything other than truth, we are walking in bondage.

If we don't hold tightly to the truth, Satan's savvy lies will convince us to loosen our grip on truth and eventually hold tightly to deception. Satan is subtle and patient. He'll plant seeds of doubt and wait for them to grow in our hearts. But if we continually fertilize our hearts with the truth of God's Word, those devilish seeds will never have a chance to sprout up as demonic weeds because they will never take root.

The Incorruptible Word of God

Keep in mind that there's nothing new under the sun. Satan doesn't have any new tricks. He is not a creative being. God is the Creator of heaven, earth and all things. Satan can only offer up a perverted counterfeit, a distorted copy, a tainted forgery. Just look at the New Age movement. When it comes to getting people to believe his lies, one of Satan's key strategies is simply to copy a principle Jesus taught His disciples in the Parable of the Sower. Let's take a look at what Jesus said in Matthew 13:

"A farmer went out to sow his seed. As he was scattering the seed, some fell along the path, and the birds came and ate it up. Some fell on rocky places, where it did not have much soil. It sprang up quickly, because the soil was shallow. But when the sun came up, the plants were scorched, and they withered because they had no root. Other seed fell among thorns, which grew up and choked the plants. Still other seed fell on good soil, where it produced a crop—a hundred, sixty or thirty times what was sown. He who has ears, let him hear."

—Matthew 13:3-9 NIV

Jesus was talking about sowing the Word of God and the different types of soils it falls upon. But keep in mind that the subject of this passage is not the soils but the seed. The Word is the incorruptible seed of God. In this parable, the seed is looking for good soil in which it can take root and flourish. When the Word of God finds a heart full of faith, it can produce an abundant harvest according to the type of seed sown.

For example, if it is the Word of God on the matter of His healing power, it will produce a harvest of healing when it is sown in a heart full of faith. (You can fill your heart full of faith by meditating on the Word.) If it is the Word of God on the matter of God's ability to provide our needs according to His riches in glory by Christ Jesus, it will produce a harvest of provision (Philippians 4:19). Of course, the Word needs both faith and patience to produce its harvest. You wouldn't expect a mustard seed to break through the soil and grow into a large tree overnight, or even after a few weeks. The Word takes time to work, but it never returns to God void. It always accomplishes what it was sent to do (Isaiah 55:11). The devil's only hope is to keep us from holding tightly to the truth until we see the manifested promise.

So what does Satan do? He tries to corrupt the incorruptible seed by sowing his own seeds of doubt, worry, fear, unbelief, and the like. If you want to learn more on how Satan uses subtle forms of doubt to rob your prayer answers, your peace, and your destiny, pick up my book "Doubtless: Faith that Overcomes the World."

The Parable of the Demonic Sower

Let's look more closely at the Parable of the Sower. When we do, we'll discover evidence that Satan got ahead of the sower and scattered his skeptical seeds as far and wide as he could. In some cases, Satan has been working the fields of our minds for years, even decades, and has erected strongholds that keep us from receiving—or even recognizing—the pure truth.

Oh, sure, we might mentally ascent that the Word of God is true in a certain area. But faith without corresponding action is dead. The actions that follow our words ultimately demonstrate what we believe. Think about it for a minute. If Sally really believes she has more than enough, then why is she so stingy come offering time? If John pled the blood of Jesus over his children, why does he have a panic attack when they are late coming home at night?

Satan isn't going to stand idly by and allow people to manifest Kingdom principles at his expense. He's too prideful to sit still and watch God get the glory in your life. He wants the glory for himself, and the only way for him to get that glory is for you to spend your days whining about how the devil is blocking your healing, or how the devil is stealing your finances, or how the devil is wreaking havoc on your relationships. (You don't see Jesus complaining to the apostles all the time about how the Pharisees were twisting His words. Yet we are so quick to complain over such silly stuff.) The devil gets the glory when we walk in his deception rather than holding tightly to God's truth. What a shame for believers to glorify the enemy in our speaking, walking, and living rather than glorifying the One who willingly endured suffering and death that we might live victorious Christian lives.

Let's take a look at Jesus' interpretation of the Parable of the Sower. As you read these passages, pay close attention to Satan's work and consider how he may be getting inroads into your own heart.

> "When anyone hears the message about the kingdom and does not understand it, the evil one comes and snatches away what was sown in his heart. This is the seed sown along the path."

—Matthew 13:19 (NIV)

So we see that Satan is actively opposing the Word of truth. He doesn't want it to get planted in our hearts to begin with because once it's planted, there's a possibility of a harvest. Remember, the harvest brings God glory. A failed crop satisfies the devils' pride. I always wondered how Satan can snatch a word that was sown in our hearts. Consider the meaning of the word snatch: "to attempt to seize something suddenly, to take or grasp abruptly or hastily; to seize or take suddenly without permission."

Don't Give the Devil Permission

When you see the full meaning of snatch, you recognize the power in it. The devil doesn't ask permission, and he doesn't wait until we've tightened our belt of truth or lifted our shield of faith to move in on our minds. He just slithers in and takes the Word of God by force—if we don't understand it. That's why it's important to meditate on the Word of God.

Anyone can read the word and receive information. Receiving revelation depends on our active pursuit of the logos (written word) until it becomes rhema (spoken word) to us. As we meditate on the Word, thinking about it, speaking it, and being doers of it, we gain spiritual understanding that keeps the devil from forcibly taking the Word from our hearts.

But I didn't answer my own question, did I? How does Satan snatch away the Word that was sown in our hearts? One way is by distracting us. If you hear an awesome message and you are pressing into this truth, Satan will come with some offence, some temptation, some distraction that aims to take our focus off the Word. When we begin to think, speak and walk toward the distraction, the devil roams in our direction and devours the Word in our hearts. Victorious Christian living means holding tightly to the truth despite the smoke and mirrors.

Although no on can snatch you out of the Father's hand (John 10:28-29), the devil can snatch the Word out of your heart. Deny the devil permission to rob your harvest by developing the habit of staying focused during church, spending time studying and meditating on God's Word on your own, and immediately putting into practice what you've learned.

Are You Rooted in Love?

Some of the sower's seed also fell on rocky places. Jesus likened the rocky places to the man who hears the Word and at once receives it with joy. But since he has no root, he lasts only a short time. When trouble or persecution comes because of the Word, he quickly falls away (Matthew 13: 20-21).

Can you see the devil in this? Think about it for a minute. Where do you think the trouble or persecution comes from? If the devil can't snatch the Word out of your heart by distracting you, he'll send trouble and persecution your way in some way, shape of form—it may even come through other Christians who are Scripturally ignorant or just plain jealous.

How are you going to respond when trouble and persecution comes? Again, the clear answer is to hold tightly to the truth. The truth is this: God loves you and nothing is ever going to change that. No man, no enemy can take away from you. But you have to be convinced of that reality. This may seem like Christianity 101—and it is—but I submit to you that if we really understood the love of Christ we would behave differently toward Him, toward ourselves and toward others.

Paul reminds, "Who will separate us from the love of Christ? Will tribulation, or distress, or persecution, or famine, or nakedness, or peril, or sword?" (Romans 8) Let's set the record straight. The answer to Paul's question is not "the devil." The devil cannot separate us from the love of Christ. The answer is not death, nor life, nor angels, nor principalities, nor powers, nor things present, nor things to come, nor height, nor depth, nor any other creature. Nothing can separate us from the love of Christ. Nothing. Nada. No, in all our troubles, tests, trials and persecutions, the Bible says were are more than conquerors through Christ Jesus. Hallelujah!

When trouble and persecution comes, our first response is to rely on God's love. We need to be rooted and grounded in God's love. We need to know the love of Christ, which passes mere knowledge without experience, so we can be filled with all the fullness of God (Ephesians 3:7-19).

As we've received Christ Jesus the Lord, we are supposed to walk in Him: Rooted and built up in Him, and established in the faith, as we have been taught, and abounding with thanksgiving. We are supposed to beware, lest any main spoil us through philosophy and vain deceit, after the traditions of men, after the rudiments of the world, and not after Christ (Colossians 2:6-8). Again, we are supposed to hold tightly to the truth.

When Trouble Comes

I don't want to be the bearer of bad news, so I'll let Paul do it. Paul told Timothy that anybody who decides to live a godly life in Christ will suffer persecutions (2 Timothy 3:12). (Notice the word "persecution" is plural, indicating it's not a one-time event.) Of course, that's not really bad news because we are assured the victory—and the persecution only makes us stronger.

If you are committed to living a victorious Christian life, then just accept the truth ahead of time that there will be persecution. I'm not suggesting that we become pessimistic by any means. I'm just suggesting we understand the whole counsel of the Word of God as it relates to persecution. Remember, Jesus said:

> "Verily I say unto you, There is no
> man that hath left house, or brethren,

or sisters, or father, or mother, or wife, or children, or lands, for my sake, and the gospel's, But he shall receive an hundredfold now in this time, houses, and brethren, and sisters, and mothers, and children, and lands, with persecutions; and in the world to come eternal life."

—Mark 10:29-30

Tribulation will come. Persecution will come. Temptation will come. Trials will come. We must be patient in tribulation (Romans 12:2). But don't accept it in defeat—and don't give in to fear. Consider what Jesus has to say about the matter:

"In the world you have tribulation and trials and distress and frustration; but be of good cheer [take courage; be confident, certain, undaunted]! For I have overcome the world. [I have deprived it of power to harm you and have conquered it for you.]"

—John 16:33 AMP

When trouble or persecution arises because of the Word, we should take courage. We should not cast away our confidence in Him. We shouldn't let the devil see us sweat because it's a sign of his perdition and our salvation (Philippians 1:28). We should hold tightly to the truth—and speak it out of our mouths. We should be confessing the truth about the love of God to combat the fear. We should be confessing the truth that we are more than conquerors through Christ Jesus (Romans 8:37). We should be confessing the truth that greater is He that is in us than he that is in the world (1 John 4:4). We should confess the truth that applies to our situation—and there's a Word for every challenge we'll ever face.

Jesus said He overcame the world (John 16:33). Have you ever thought about how Jesus overcame the world? If we can discover how Jesus overcame the world then we can overcome the world, too.

Remember, God came to earth as a man, anointed with the Holy Ghost and power. God has made the same Holy Ghost and power available to us. But Jesus had more than just the Holy Ghost and power—He had faith. And this is the victory that overcomes the world—even our faith (1 John 5:4). The good news is, we have the measure of faith. We are overcomers, fully equipped to overcome in every trial. Beyond all of this, Scripture offers a clear response to trials of any kind: rejoice. When we are secure in His love for us, we can rejoice with sincerity. Paul told us by the Holy Spirit to rejoice in the truth (1 Corinthians 13:6). Rejoice!

Don't Be a Worry Wart

Jesus spoke of yet another strategy of the enemy to steal the truth from us. It seems when the devil is not able to snatch the Word out of our hearts, he has a plan B. Plan B involves choking the Word out of us. Jesus said this happens when the worries of life and the deceitfulness of riches supersede the truth, making it unfruitful.

> "Then the cares and anxieties of the world and distractions of the age, and the pleasure and delight and false glamour and deceitfulness of riches, and the craving and passionate desire for other things creep in and choke and suffocate the Word, and it becomes fruitless."
>
> —Mark 4:19 (AMP)

In other words, instead of holding tightly to the truth and keeping steady on the middle of the road, this person goes off into one of three miry ditches: (1) wondering how he'll solve his problems; (2) thinking money is the answer to everything; or (3) hot pursuit of something other than the Kingdom of God and His righteousness.

The Fruitful Soil

But alas, it is possible for the seed sown to bear fruit—and abundant fruit—if it lands on good soil in the heart. Mark 4:20 says the one who received the seed that fell on good soil is the man who hears the Word and understands it. He produces a crop, yielding 100, 60 or 30 times what was sown. I like the Message translation of this Verse: "But the seed planted in the good earth represents those who hear the Word, embrace it, and produce a harvest beyond their wildest dreams."

I don't know about you, but I have some pretty wild dreams! I don't know about you, but I'm counting on the Word of God that says, "No eye has seen, no ear has heard, and no mind has imagined what God has prepared for those who love him" (1 Corinthians 2:9 NLT). And again, He is able to do immeasurably more than all we ask or imagine, according to His power that is at work within us (Ephesians 3:20). I want to make an impact in this world for God—but I have to continue the habit of holding tightly to the truth because the devil wants to snatch it out of my heart with his subtle deceptions. The same holds true for you. How do you cultivate good soil in your heart? Embrace the Word! Put another way, consider carefully what you hear and, by the grace of God, walk in the truth you receive. When you do that consistently, over time you will see a harvest of fruit in your life.

After He explained the Parable of the Sower, Jesus said something interesting:

> "Be careful what you are hearing. The measure [of thought and study] you give [to the truth you hear] will be the measure [of virtue and knowledge] that comes back to you--and more [besides] will be given to you who hear."

> —Mark 4:24 (AMP)

If we give care and thought to what we are hearing; if we consider and reflect and meditate on the Word of truth, that Word will take root in our hearts and begin to renew our minds. I believe that the more our minds are renewed, the easier it becomes to receive and walk in additional truth that takes us deeper in God.

For example, if you don't have a revelation of the unconditional love of God, it may be harder to receive the truth of God's forgiveness for your mistakes. Without a revelation of His grace, mercy and love, the devil can heap condemnation on you and make it difficult to receive His total forgiveness. By contrast, if you have a revelation of who you are in Christ, then you will be more able to receive truths about the healing power of God and your inheritance in Him. When you have the right roots, you can endure the trials and live in victory on the inside no matter what your circumstances look like on the outside. And the devils on the outside have to bow to the Jesus on the inside of you. Glory to God!

Beyond carefully considering what you hear, you can prepare the soil of your heart for the promised harvest by staying focused on what God has called you to do and not worrying about what anyone else is doing. Even if you are the only person in your family who's staying on the straight and narrow—and even if they seem to be prospering when you aren't—don't let that worry you or distract you. Don't let it choke the good seed planted in your heart. In short, guard your heart more than anything else, because the source of your life flows from it (Proverbs 4:23 GOD's Word Translation).

Paul's Truthful Warnings

There's another point I need to make as it relates to holding tightly to the truth (2 Timothy 1:13-14). We need to make sure we're holding to it in the context of the whole canon of Scripture. Unfortunately, some have based doctrines on a single verse that actually contradicts the truth. This is often the case when new fads roll through the Body of Christ.

Paul exhorted Timothy to show himself approved of God, a workman that need not to be ashamed, rightly dividing the word of truth (2 Timothy 2:15). Paul went on to warn Timothy about what happens to those who do not hold tightly to the truth: they fall by the wayside like Phygelus and Hermongenes. Victorious Christians maintain a healthy balance between new revelation and solid foundations. In this way, we move forward in the progressive truth that God is revealing while never straying from the foundational doctrines of Christ that ground us in Kingdom reality. If we aren't students of the Word, we could unknowingly trade trendy dogma for an eternal certainty. We could even deny the truth.

Paul didn't patty cake around the dangers of denying the truth. It would have been irresponsible not to make the consequences of defying the Word abundantly clear. That's why Paul warned that the wrath of God is revealed from heaven against all ungodliness and unrighteousness of men, who hold the truth in unrighteousness (Romans 1:8). He talked of those who changed the truth of God into a lie, and worshipped and served the creature more than the Creator (Romans 1:24-26). He said those who believe not the truth would be damned (2 Thessalonians 2:12).

Sometimes Paul's words seemed harsh, but he spoke the truth in love so that his spiritual children could grow up into the full stature of Jesus. Paul's desire was that a Christian's life would "lovingly express truth [in all things, speaking truly, dealing truly, living truly]. Enfolded in love, let us grow up in every way and in all things into Him Who is the Head, [even] Christ (the Messiah, the Anointed One) (Ephesians 4:15 AMP). Similarly, Paul's desire for the lost was that they might be saved and come to the knowledge of the truth (1 Timothy 2:4).

Paul knew that after he went on to be with the Lord, Timothy, and others into whom he poured his life, would remain to take the truth of the Gospel to the lost. He told Timothy like it was, urging him to guard his own heart, to guard the truth, and to teach it to others. Victorious Christian living demands that we take Paul's words to heart—to obey the truth through the Spirit so that we may be firmly rooted and established in truth. If we don't hold fast to the truth, we can't lead others in its way. Even worse still, we might also find ourselves in the clutches of deception. The blind will lead the blind and all will fall into a devilish ditch. It's the truth that sets us free, and we need to continually seek it as if our lives depended on it—because they do.

The Truth Starts with You

Let's bring all of this home. Victorious Christian living demands walking in truth and talking in truth, or, as the Amplified Bible put it earlier, "speaking truly, dealing truly, and living truly." The world is watching. You may be the only example of truth in the lives of some. If you are walking in darkness in any area of your life, you aren't walking in the fullness of the truth. If you are speaking doubt and unbelief out of your mouth, you aren't talking in the fullness of the truth. If you are praising God on Sunday and cursing your co-workers on Monday, you are not living in the fullness of the truth. Don't compromise the Kingdom in your life. Seek it first and always.

Have you ever testified in court? The clerk comes up to you, tells you to put your hand on a Bible, and asks a solemn question: "Do you swear to tell the truth, the whole truth, and nothing but the truth, so help you God?"

We need to speak our words, deal with people, and live our lives accordingly. We need to speak, walk, and live as if God is watching our every move—because He is. If we want to be a credible witness for Jesus Christ, if we want the anointing of the Holy Spirit and power on our lives, if we want to please God, it takes more than faith alone. If we want to finish strong, we need truth in the inward parts (Psalm 51:6). We all make mistakes. There's grace for that. I'm talking about setting our standards where God sets His and being quick to repent when we miss it. It's not about being perfect. It's about our heart attitude. A humble heart toward a loving God is a testimony to a lost world so full of pride.

Breakthrough Exercise: Seeking the Truth

American Writer William F. Buckley, Jr., once said, "Truth is a demure lady, much too ladylike to knock you on your head and drag you to her cave. She is there, but people must want her, and seek her out."

When you are seeking the Kingdom of God and His righteousness, truth is part of what you are seeking. Seek the truth in all things and you will be well on your way to a victorious Christian life. Consider this action exercise that will help you see a 30-, 60- or 100-fold harvest in your life.

1. Are there questions you have about issues going on in your life? Struggles you are having that you don't understand how to deal with? Maybe a loved one died and you don't understand why God didn't heal them. Maybe your spouse left you and you are devastated. Maybe your kids are in deep trouble and you feel you've failed as a parent. Rather than doubting—or even getting mad with God like I did so many years ago—take the time to seek the truth on these matters. The truth, once accepted and acted upon, will eventually bring the change in your life that you are longing for. Your job is to find the truth and continue in it. Don't let distractions, offenses, or anything else choke the word out of your heart.

2. Pray and ask the Holy Spirit to show you any areas of your life where you are believing something that is not true or where you may be misinterpreting Scripture. Then be open to what He might show you. If He shows you something, go to the Word of God and study it out to show yourself approved, then stick with the unadulterated truth you find.

3. Ask the Holy Sprit to help you walk in the truth. He will lead you and guide you into all truth (John 16:13). Pay attention to His promptings.

4. Determine in your heart not to worry or fret. Cast your cares on Him because He cares for you. (1 Peter 5:7). This was my biggest struggle. If I wasn't reasoning I was worrying. But humility casts the care on the Lord and trusts in His goodness, His wisdom and His power. You can't be a victorious Christian if you are consumed with worry and fret.

CHAPTER 5

Victory Habit #4
Stay Focused on Christ

Remember that Jesus Christ of the seed of David was raised from the dead according to my gospel...

—2 Timothy 2:8

Victorious Christian living means preserving and standing your ground with patience to endure anything and everything for the sake of the Gospel. In order to do that, we have to stay focused. We have to keep the main thing the main thing—and the main thing is Jesus.

Jesus is our King and our Lord. He is the Chief Cornerstone to which we all must align if we want to grow to His full stature. When we stay focused on Jesus, what He wants to do, and how He wants to do it, we will find the grace we need to run the race set before us. We will live victorious Christian lives.

Jesus is Alive!

We opened this chapter with Paul's instructions to Timothy to remember the resurrected Christ. Now, let's look at the Message translation of 2 Timothy 2:8-9: "Fix this picture firmly in your mind: Jesus, descended from the line of David, raised from the dead. It's what you've heard from me all along."

Paul gave Timothy a very clear instruction: Stay focused on Jesus. Meditate on the truth that Jesus was raised from the dead. Visualize Jesus as alive, even though you haven't seen Him with your own two eyes.

Paul was painting a powerful picture of Jesus as a living God. If Jesus wasn't raised from the dead, then there would be no Good News to preach. Paul would have no Gospel to take to the Gentiles. Please don't glaze over this! It is absolutely vital that we see Jesus as alive—and not just alive, but seated at the right hand of the Father making intercession for us 24/7/365 (Hebrews 7:25).

Stop and think about this for a minute. Even as you read the words on this page, Jesus is literally sitting next to the Father interceding on your behalf. Sure, you may have friends who are faithful to stand in the gap and make up the hedge. We all need faithful friends in this world. But there is no friend like Jesus! He never grows weary and He knows how to get prayer answers! He died for you and He has a vested interest in seeing you live a victorious Christian life to the glory of God.

Let's stay in this flow for another minute. There is power in this Word and we need to draw from the truth in these verses as we seek victory in every area of our lives. Again, the Bible says Jesus always lives to intercede for you (Hebrews 7:25). When you sin, Jesus is there to intercede for you. When you need a breakthrough, Jesus is there to intercede for you. Whatever you need to live according to His perfect plan for your life, Jesus is there to intercede for you. God supplies all of your needs according to His glorious riches in Christ Jesus (Philippians 4:19).

What Will You Magnify?

Armed with this truth, why would you want to focus on your problems? You empower in your emotions what you focus on in your mind. I implore you by the mercies of God, stop thinking and talking about your problems! Whatever you focus on is magnified in your life, so focus on the resurrected Christ.

When we keep our focus on the resurrected Christ, it builds faith in our hearts that we are not in this battle alone—and that we can walk in victory. Remember, Jesus overcame the world. We can thank Father God that He leads us along in Christ's triumphal procession (2 Corinthians 2:14). Hallelujah!

But wait—it gets even better. When we focus on the resurrected Christ, we can't help but remember how He was resurrected. Jesus was resurrected by the power of the Holy Spirit. And guess what? The Spirit that raised Christ from the dead dwells in us (Romans 8:11). (That's shouting ground right there!) The power that raised Christ from the dead works in us to accomplish His will. When we focus on the resurrected Christ—when we magnify Him instead of our problems—we'll see Him living in victory and we'll see ourselves living victorious lives in Him. Believe me, I understand that sometimes it's difficult to remember to focus on Christ when people are questioning your calling, when fear is attacking your mind, when you don't feel well, or when you are facing various other types of trials. But if Timothy can do it, so can you. Timothy had challenges in his day. His mother a Jew. His father a Gentile. That sort of union didn't go over too well back then—and that wasn't Timothy's only challenge.

Timothy's Tall Task

After he was called into ministry, Timothy had to deal with people who thought he was too young to lead the church (1 Timothy 4:12). He had to deal with his own fears (2 Timothy 1:7). And apparently he had some trouble with his stomach and got sick quite often (1 Timothy 5:23).

Timothy could have focused on his youth, his anxiety or his belly ache, but he chose to focus on Christ. Because he stayed focused on Christ, we find him repeatedly serving with Paul on his Gospel-preaching journeys. Timothy helped Paul change the known world in their day and went on to continue Paul's work after the apostle departed his earthly tent.

Paul knew that Timothy would need to keep in mind the power of Christ's resurrection in order to handle the challenges that went along with spreading the Gospel in his day. Paul knew that in order for Timothy to maintain the strength he needed to fight—and win—the good fight of faith for himself, he'd need to keep his mind on a resurrected Jesus.

Isaiah put it this way: "Thou wilt keep him in perfect peace, whose mind is stayed on thee: because he trusteth in thee" (Isaiah 26:3). When we stay focused on Jesus—who He really is and how much He loves us—we will find peace and power that always causes us to triumph. Thanks be to God!

Timothy learned to do this. Tradition tells us that Timothy died a martyr's death. Timothy was reportedly found protesting against the lewd acts that were part of a heathen carnival. An angry mob beat him to death with clubs. Timothy stood fearlessly, keeping in mind the resurrected Christ. If God's grace is sufficient for Timothy to face an angry mob with clubs, it's sufficient for us to overcome every obstacle to victorious Christian living.

Transformed into His Image

Of course, Timothy didn't start off with such boldness. He had to be transformed into the image of Christ in order to find the strength to confront the sin in the land. Paul knew that Timothy would become more Christ-like if he kept his focus on Jesus. Paul equipped Timothy for his destiny with sound advice he could meditate on over and over.

No doubt, Paul taught Timothy much of the truth he shared with other churches as they traveled together on apostolic missions. Over and over, Timothy probably heard wisdom like this:

"And all of us, as with unveiled face, [because we] continued to behold [in the Word of God] as in a mirror the glory of the Lord, are constantly being transfigured into His very own image in ever increasing splendor and from one degree of glory to another; [for this comes] from the Lord [Who is] the Spirit."

—2 Corinthians 3:18 (AMP)

We may not know for sure who wrote the book of Hebrews, however we do know that this writer knew Timothy because Timothy is mentioned in the letter (Hebrews 13:23). That means Timothy was likely exposed to wisdom that suggested we "throw off everything that hinders us, to strip off and throw aside every unnecessary weight and any sin that has us tangled up so we can run with patient endurance and steady and active persistence the appointed course of the race that is set before us" (Hebrews 12:1).

Timothy had to strip off what others thought about him. Timothy had to strip off his own anxieties. Timothy had to strip off the fact that he hadn't received healing for his oft infirmities. Timothy probably had to strip off plenty in order to run with a fast-paced Paul. We know that John

Mark couldn't keep up with the apostle in their early journeys. Timothy had probably heard about the John Mark incident and wondered if he could live up to the task of traveling to the nations with this bold apostle.

How did Timothy do it? The writer of Hebrews offers some insight:

> "Looking away [from all that will distract] to Jesus, Who is the Leader and the Source of our faith [giving the first incentive for our belief] and is also its Finisher [bringing it to maturity and perfection]."

> —Hebrews 12:2 (AMP)

Lessons from the Line of David

Timothy had to stay focused on Christ. Not Paul. Not himself. Not his mixed heritage. Christ and Christ alone. Timothy had a good role model in David, who was also called into ministry at a young age. David made it a habit to keep his eyes on God. He said things like, "Mine eyes are ever toward the Lord; for he shall pluck my feet out of the net" (Psalm 25:15). And again, "For thy lovingkindness is before mine eyes: and I have walked in thy truth" (Psalm 26:3). And again, "I will set no wicked thing before mine eyes" (Psalm 101:3). When David faced battles, he looked for the Lord of Hosts—and he always found Him. Victorious Christian living demands the same mindset that was in David, and later found to be in Timothy.

Solomon, David's son and successor to the throne, also learned to keep his eyes on God— and he scribed that wisdom in Proverbs so generations to come would be encouraged to do the same. Consider some of the Spirit-inspired words of Solomon:

> "My son, attend to my words; incline thine ear unto my sayings. Let them not depart from thine eyes; keep them in the midst of thine heart. For they are life unto those that find them, and health to all their flesh."

> —Proverbs 4:20-22

Jesus Himself gave us clear instruction about where our focus should be: "Seek (aim at and strive after) first of all His kingdom and His righteousness (His way of doing and being right), and then all these things taken together will be given you besides" (Matthew 6:33 AMP).

The bottom line: We need to stay focused on Christ, what He wants to do, and how He wants to do it—and the fact that we have resurrection power dwelling in us to accomplish His will in every situation. If we lose our focus, we put ourselves at risk of not completing the work the Lord has given us to do. If we lose our focus, we won't walk in the fullness of the victorious Christian life Jesus died to give us.

Let me put this another way: God doesn't like it when we let persecution stop us because He's given us clear instructions on how to respond to persecution. God doesn't like it when we let fear stop us because He's told us how to face down fear. God doesn't like it when we let sickness stop us because He's taught us what to do when sickness strikes.

God doesn't expect us never to stumble and His grace abounds when we do. He just expects us to set our minds to stay focused on His Word, a source of instruction on victorious Christian living. He's given us the measure of faith to live the life. He has made us co-laborers with Christ. Let's stay focused.

The Power of Focus

There is power in focus. Filmmaker Alan Pariser once said, "The sun's energy warms the world. But when you focus it through a magnifying glass it can start a fire. Focus is so powerful!"

If you focus on Jesus, you'll stay on fire for Him. You'll have fervent faith that will serve as a defense against the enemy's attacks. (Check out my book "Fervent Faith: Discover how a fervent spirit is a defense against the devil" for more information on this defense.)

Two contrasting Bible texts come to mind that demonstrate the power of focus, for better or worse. The first one comes from the Old Testament. You remember the story. God told Moses to send a leader from each tribe of Israel to spy out the Promised Land. They came back and told Moses, Aaron, and all the congregation of the children of Israel that the land was fruitful and flowing with milk and honey, just as God said it would be. It should have been a time of revival. Instead, it was a sad day for most of Israel.

> "Caleb tried to quiet the people as they stood before Moses. 'Let's go at once to take the land,' he said. 'We can certainly conquer it!'

> "But the other men who had explored the land with him disagreed. 'We can't go up against them! They are stronger than we are!' So they spread this bad report about the land among the Israelites:

'The land we traveled through and explored will devour anyone who goes to live there. All the people we saw were huge. We even saw giants there, the descendants of Anak. Next to them we felt like grasshoppers, and that's what they thought, too!'"

—Numbers 13:30-33 NLT

At this news, the whole community began weeping aloud and they cried all night. Israel was in an uproar and started protesting against Moses and Aaron. The children of Israel must have had a memory lapse because they actually suggested they would have been better off dying in Egypt than facing the giants in Canaan. It wasn't long before the Israelites started plotting to choose a new leader and return to slavery in Egypt.

The truth of the matter is, their leader was ultimately God. My, how quickly they were willing to forsake Him to return to the bondage of Egypt. After 40 years of wandering around aimlessly, grumbling and complaining, Israel was finally on the brink of its breakthrough. And now they were going to give it all up to go back into utter bondage. All because they were focused on the wrong thing.

After witnessing decades of miracles day in and day out, this response is astonishing. But it shows the power of focus.

The Israelites were focusing on the oversized Gentiles instead of focusing on their covenant-keeping God. They were focusing on the ominous giants instead of focusing on their omnipotent God.

But let's dig a little deeper here. The real root of Israel's failure wasn't really focusing on the giants. That was just a byproduct. The real root of this Bible history-making failure was that God's people were focusing on themselves instead of focusing on God.

Focusing on ourselves (and focusing on our giant circumstances) brings us into a land flowing with fear and doubt rather than into a land flowing with milk and honey. It's tempting when we face opposition to look at our own resources, compare them to the problem, decide we're doomed, and look for somewhere to run and hide (even back into bondage). But victorious Christian living defies the temptation to run from the battle line. Like David, when we focus on God we will not hesitate to run to the battle line because we are assured the victory in Christ. The truth is—and what you should focus on—is that your Goliath is already defeated. Whatever pseudonym Goliath is using—be it IRS issues, health hazards, family fiascos, and so on—it can't stand against the Word of God released in faith.

David Runs to the Battle Line

Doubtless, David read the story of Joshua and Caleb; how they were willing to stand on the Word of God to take the Promised Land despite the fearful sentiment in the camp. David knew all too well how Joshua led Israel into victory at Jericho and how Caleb later took a mountain in his old age. Compared to an army of giants, then, who was Goliath but one oversized man, outside the covenant of God? Can see how God's Word will change your perspective?

God said Caleb had a "different spirit" than the rest of the Israelites who treated Him with contempt by not listening to His voice. David also had a different spirit. These men were emboldened by their focus on God and His Word. They didn't carry the world's perspective. They had God's thoughts on the matter and as they stayed focused on God's will they were empowered to accomplish His will.

I wonder if David was thinking about Caleb's bold declaration—"Let's go at once to take the land. We can certainly conquer it!"—when he witnessed his fellow Israelites unwilling to face down Goliath. I wonder if David could see the parallels between ancient Israel's fear of facing many giants and his contemporaries' fear of facing a single giant. One thing is certain: David saw his God as bigger than the giant. Can you say the same?

Goliath the Midget

As the story goes, the Philistines drew up their troops for battle. Saul and the Israelites prepared for battle on the opposite hill. There was a valley in between the two opposing armies. Israel may have been feeling pretty confident, given their track record for success in battle—until they saw a horrifying sight that took their focus off of God's delivering power. (The following recount draws from language in the Message Bible.)

> "A giant nearly 10 feet tall stepped out from the Philistine line into the open, Goliath from Gath. He had a bronze helmet on his head and was dressed in armor—126 pounds of it! He wore bronze shin guards and carried a bronze sword. His spear was like a fence rail—the spear tip alone weighed over 15 pounds. His shield bearer walked ahead of him.

> Goliath stood there and called out to the Israelite troops, 'Why bother using your whole army? Am I not Philistine enough for you? And

you're all committed to Saul, aren't you? So pick your best fighter and pit him against me. If he gets the upper hand and kills me, the Philistines will all become your slaves. But if I get the upper hand and kill him, you'll all become our slaves and serve us. I challenge the troops of Israel this day. Give me a man. Let us fight it out together!'

When Saul and his troops heard the Philistine's challenge, they were terrified and lost all hope."

—1 Samuel 17: 4-11

See, Saul and his troops weren't focused on the power of Almighty God. They weren't looking at Him. They weren't meditating on His Word. They were doing just what their ancestors did: looking at the giant in the land. The only difference is the Israelites in the wilderness were facing many giants. Saul and his troops were facing but one. But the moral of the story remains the same: Focusing on the giant (the circumstance) will ultimately leave you terrified and without hope if you don't think you can conquer it yourself.

The problem is, you can't conquer anything yourself and you know it. Only pride would suggest that you can do anything apart from Christ. And pride comes before a fall. So this focus on self leaves you impotent. By contrast, focusing on God will allow you to draw from His omnipotence. Focusing on God will make you strong in the Lord and the power of His might. Saul's army focused on Goliath. David focused on God.

Enter David. While his three oldest brothers went to war with Saul, David went back and forth from serving to Saul to tending his father's sheep in Bethlehem. Each morning and evening for 40 days, Goliath took his stand and made his speech.

One day, David's dad told him to take some bread and wheat to his brothers at the battle line and to bring back a report about how they were faring. He arrived at the camp just as the army was moving into battle formation, shouting the war cry.

The Philistine champion, Goliath of Gath, stepped out from the front lines of the Philistines, and gave his usual challenge. David heard him. The Israelites, to a man, fell back the moment they saw the giant—totally frightened. Then David stepped up and told Saul he was willing to fight Goliath.

Despite the fact that the Israeli army was terrified of Goliath, David fearlessly volunteered to fight the giant. David wasn't focusing on the fear of his brethren any more than he was focused on the intimidating words oozing out of Goliath's foul mouth. The ruddy youth wasn't focused on himself, either. The future king remained focused on Almighty God. He remembered past victories against lions and bears that took lambs from his flock. But he didn't get prideful about those victories. He recalled how God empowered him to rescue the lamb. He remembered how God empowered him to kill the lions and bears with his own bare hands. Somehow, Goliath didn't seem all that threatening as David put himself in the hands of His God, a God of deliverance. Victorious Christian living focuses on the God of deliverance.

After refusing Saul's armor, David took his shepherd's staff, selected five smooth stones from the brook, and put them in the pocket of his shepherd's pack, and with his sling in his hand approached Goliath.

David's Supernatural Focus

As Goliath paced back and forth, his shield bearer in front of him, he noticed David. He took one look down on him and sneered—a mere youngster, apple-cheeked and peach-fuzzed.

Goliath ridiculed David. 'Am I a dog that you come after me with a stick?' And he cursed him by his gods. 'Come on,' Goliath said. 'I'll make road kill of you for the buzzards. I'll turn you into a tasty morsel for the field mice.'

David answered, 'You come at me with sword and spear and battle-ax. I come at you in the name of God-of-the-Angel-Armies, the God of Israel's troops, whom you curse and mock. This very day God is handing you over to me. I'm about to kill you, cut off your head, and serve up your body and the bodies of your Philistine buddies to the crows and coyotes. The whole earth will know that there's an extraordinary God in Israel. And everyone gathered here will learn that God doesn't save by means of sword or spear. The battle belongs to God—he's handing you to us on a platter!'"

—1 Samuel 17:45-47

Wow. That's the same spirit in which we need to address the fear that works to steal, kill, and destroy God's plans for our lives. Fear comes to take our focus off God and His Word. Fear comes to paralyze our faith. Fear comes to take us out of God's will. Fear comes to block our victory in Christ.

Whether it's a detrimental report from the doctor, a failing family life, or some other circumstantial crisis, fear comes to convince us that God's Word won't work for us. When you resist fear, it will surely flee—but it might rear its ugly head one more time on its way out the back door. And it might revisit at a more opportune time. Focus on God and fear won't stand a chance.

David's Prophetic Promise

Are you ready to shout? David's prophetic promise roused Goliath, and he started toward David. David took off from the front line, running toward the Philistine.

> "David reached into his pocket for a stone, slung it, and hit the Philistine hard in the forehead, embedding the stone deeply. The Philistine crashed, facedown in the dirt.
>
> That's how David beat the Philistine—with a sling and a stone. He hit him and killed him. No sword for David! Then David ran up to the Philistine and stood over him, pulled the giant's sword from its sheath, and finished the job by cutting off his head. When the Philistines saw that their great champion was dead, they scattered, running for their lives."

—1 Samuel 17:48-51

Victorious Christian living flies in the face of fear, runs to the battle line, and wages war in the name of the living God whose Word never fails. Of course, when you run to the battle line to meet your Goliath, the war in your mind may intensify with every step. Whether your battle line is in the workplace, on the home front, the court house, or somewhere else, you will see the ultimate victory manifest by focusing on God, keeping His Word in your mouth, and waiting on Him to deliver you.

Keep this Scripture in mind and stay focused on God:

> "Even youths shall faint and be weary, and [selected] young men shall feebly stumble and fall exhausted; But those who wait for the Lord [who expect, look for, and hope in Him] shall change and renew their strength and power; they shall lift their wings and mount up [close to God] as eagles [mount up to the sun]; they shall run and not be weary, they shall walk and not faint or become tired."

> —Isaiah 40:30-31 (AMP)

Victorious Christian living means staying focused on the Lord. We should be expecting Him, looking for Him, and hoping in Him in every situation. This mindset assures us the supernatural grace we need to face any giant with victory.

The Past is Gone

One final thought: Sometimes our past tries to drag us backward even while the Holy Spirit leads us to continue moving toward our destiny in Christ. Here again we need to focus on God, His plans and His purposes—or we won't fulfill them. Lot's wife looked back when God was calling her to the next place. Essentially, she was paralyzed. You can't move forward while you are looking back or you will keep stumbling over your past.

I'd like to share with you a powerful prophetic word that someone gave me that reminds me not to get stuck in my past. This prophetic word really spoke to me at a time in my life when I had to leave everything behind to follow God into the next place He had ordained for me. There was more victory ahead for me that I never would have attained if I kept looking back. Here is the Word:

> "Do not look back. Lot and his family were instructed to 'not look

back'... So too are you not to look back. You have been rescued, the old life destroyed. You are to continue stepping forward through new doors into fresh anointing.

Every day is new, let go of the old, let go of yesterday, let go of yester-year. Hold no longer to the past, it is done...dead...done. Look forward with hope and anticipation...step out onto the water and walk. All things ARE possible.

I provide for you daily. Fresh bread, fresh manna. Taste and see that I, the Lord, am good. Let go of the past. It was. It no longer is. Shift your thinking to the future. Ask me to stir up in you my hope and dreams. My plan as designed for you from before you were born. Nothing is impossible for me, nothing. All things are possible.

It does not matter what the past looks like. It is gone, past, no longer alive...unless you keep it alive in your mind. Shift your thinking to the future. Intentionally drown the past with thoughts of the future…of what is to come…with the hope of what will be. Believe what I have for you…your destiny has not changed. It remains and awaits you.

Looking at the past has you frozen like a pillar of salt….has you wading in the stagnant waters of the Dead Sea. The choice is yours. Look back or look forward with a hope and a future. Step into the race set before you. Step into the river of life, full of fresh living water.

Press on to the finish line, daily drinking fresh living water, daily eating fresh bread. Yesterday's bread is moldy and there is no need to eat the bread of yesterday, for daily there is fresh bread for you.

I have for you a hope and a future. Join in the race and look ahead to the goal…to hear my say, 'Well done my good and faithful servant'."

Although Paul didn't write this in his letters to Timothy, I'm sure he offered the same advice to his spiritual son that he did to the church at Philippi: "I focus on this one thing: Forgetting the past and looking forward to what lies ahead, I press on to reach the end of the race and receive the heavenly prize for which God, through Christ Jesus, is calling us" (Philippians 3:13).

Breakthrough Exercise:
Staying Focused on Christ

With the hustle and bustle of life—and with the devil working his ministry—it's easy enough to get distracted. But you can stay focused on Christ if you really want to. Put these steps into action in your life and develop laser-like focus on God.

1. Ask God for His perspective. When you wait upon the Lord, He renews your strength and gives you the perspective of an eagle (Isaiah 40:31). In other words, He lifts you above every situation and offers you a different perspective—His perspective. You don't have to look at the world through the eyes of the world. Look at the world through the eyes of Christ. And, for that matter, don't spend too much time looking at the world. That's not where your victory comes from. Paul instructed, "Set your minds on things above, not on earthly things. For you died, and your life is now hidden with Christ in God" (Colossians 3:3-4).

2. Talk to God throughout the day. Paul said, "Pray without ceasing" (1 Thessalonians 5:17). Although you can't sit and pray all day, victorious Christians have learned that you can make God part of your conversation throughout the day by just thanking Him, acknowledging Him in all your ways, and asking for and receiving grace.

3. Pray Ephesians prayers. Paul prayed two power-packed prayers over the church at Ephesus that you would do well to pray over yourself every day. I am going to share both of them with you now as modified in the first person to make it easier for you to make these prayers personal.

Ephesians 1:17-21 (NIV):

I ask you God of my Lord Jesus Christ, the glorious Father, to give me the Spirit of wisdom and revelation, so that I may know You better. I pray also that the eyes of my heart may be enlightened in order that I may know the hope to which You have called me, the riches of Your glorious inheritance in the saints, and Your incomparably great power for me who believes. That power is like the working of Your mighty strength, which You exerted in Christ when

You raised Him from the dead and seated Him at Your right hand in the heavenly realms, far above all rule and authority, power and dominion, and every title that can be given, not only in the present age but also in the one to come. And You placed all things under Jesus' feet and appointed Him to be head over everything for the church, which is His body, the fullness of him who fills everything in every way.

Ephesians 3:15-21 (NIV):

Father, from whom Your whole family in heaven and on earth derives its name, I pray that out of Your glorious riches You may strengthen me with power through Your Spirit in my inner being, so that Christ may dwell in my heart through faith. And I pray that as I am rooted and established in love, I may have power, together with all the saints, to grasp how wide and long and high and deep is the love of Christ, and know this love that surpasses knowledge—that I may be filled to the measure of all the fullness of God. Now to him who is able to do immeasurably more than all we ask or imagine, according to His power that is at work within me, to Him be glory in the church and in Christ Jesus throughout all generations, for ever and ever! Amen.

Pray these prayers over yourself every day. You will see the fruit of this Word-based prayer in your life manifest in the form of a deeper knowledge of who you are in Christ—and a stronger focus on Christ in your life.

CHAPTER 6

Effective Habit #5
Bearing the Fruit of Discipline

I don't think there's any comparison between the present hard times and the coming good times. The created world itself can hardly wait for what's coming next.

—Romans 8:18-19

Paul didn't sugarcoat victorious Christian living. Remember, victorious Christian living isn't necessarily sitting in TBN's studio doing an interview with one of the Crouches. Victorious Christian living isn't necessarily teaching the Word of God to tens of thousands of people in an arena. Victorious Christian living is doing what God has called you to do—whether that's preaching the Gospel to the nations, raising your children in the admonition and fear of the Lord, conquering the marketplace, or something else— and doing it for the glory of God. That may or may not be glamorous, but it always comes with great rewards.

No, Paul didn't sugarcoat victorious Christian living. He told Timothy straight up that he'd need a good habit called self-discipline to live the victorious Christian life and fulfill his destiny. Self-discipline runs through the same vein as self-control, a fruit of the Spirit that results from following the Holy Spirit's lead to crucify the flesh. Consider Paul's words to Timothy:

> "Take [with me] your share of the hardships and suffering [which you are called to endure] as a good (first-class) soldier of Christ Jesus. No soldier when in service gets entangled in the enterprises of [civilian] life; his aim is to satisfy and please the one who enlisted him."

> —2 Timothy 2:3-4 (AMP)

In other words, don't let the world complicate your life and ministry. Stay focused on what you are called to do. Discipline yourself to play by the rules that God has laid down. Submit your life to the Word of God even if you have to suffer along the way. Ultimately, our lives on this earth a flash in the eternal pan. It's a few decades compared to time without end. Take the eternal view.

Self-Control: A Fruit of the Spirit

Victorious Christian living demands discipline and self-control. Now, there's self-control we can exercise by the grace of God and there's the discipline, or chastening, of the Lord. You get to choose which road you'll travel, and you're sure to spend some time on each path. But if you choose self-control you'll meet with much less chastening. It's sort of like humility. If you humble yourself, God won't have to. But if you walk in pride, you'll find humbling experiences along your path.

I'd rather cooperate with the Holy Spirit to bear the fruit of self-control than have the Lord find need to discipline me. But even if the Lord does discipline me, I know it's for my own good. The writer of Hebrews explained, "No discipline seems pleasant at the time, but painful. Later on, however, it produces a harvest of righteousness and peace for those who have been trained by it" (Hebrews 12:11).

Admittedly, discipline tends to be painful whether it comes from the Lord or whether we impose it on ourselves. That's because our flesh wants to do what our flesh wants to do. The mind of the flesh is enmity against God (Romans 8:7).

The sinful nature desires what is contrary to the Spirit, and the Spirit what is contrary to the sinful nature (Galatians 5:17). But Paul learned how to crucify his flesh, and he taught Timothy—and us—how to be of the same mind. Paul said:

> "I always exercise and discipline myself [mortifying my body, deadening my carnal affections, bodily appetites, and worldly desires, endeavoring in all respects] to have a clear (unshaken, blameless) conscience, void of offense toward God and toward men."
>
> —Acts 24:15-17 (AMP)

Discipline and suffering often go hand in hand. But the rewards are great. I tell you the truth: Victorious Christian living means suffering the pain of self-discipline even when people around you seem to be on an easy ride. Yes, we believe that we receive. But many times it is determined, disciplined faith that wins the battle for God's manifested promises in our life. Our job is not to compare our path to another's. Our job is to agree with the Word, believe God, yield to the Holy Spirit, and make disciplined choices; choices like studying the Word, going to church, praying fervently, and obeying God in our every day lives.

Greek Philosopher Plato said, "The first and best victory is to conquer self." You need mental toughness and a heavy load of God's grace to conquer self. Grace is the power of God working in us to change us from glory to glory. But what is mental toughness? Vince Lombardi, one of the most victorious football coaches of all time, said, "Mental toughness is many things and rather difficult to explain. Its qualities are sacrifice and self-denial. Also, most importantly, it is combined with a perfectly disciplined will that refuses to give in. It's a state of mind—you could call it character in action."

Victorious Christian living demands character in action. The good news, as I've said repeatedly, is that you don't have to discipline yourself in your own strength. You just have to be willing. Paul wanted to make sure Timothy knew that. That's why he told his spiritual son, "God did not give us a spirit of timidity, but a spirit of power, of love and of self-discipline" (2 Timothy 1:7 NIV). Self-discipline is part of our spiritual DNA. We have to rely on the Spirit of Grace, and set our mind, will and emotions on His will, to live a disciplined life. And a disciplined life is a victorious life.

Suffering Gracefully

Paul told Timothy to willingly take his share of the suffering he was called to endure. We, too, must be willing to take our share of suffering as soldiers for Christ. Indeed, victorious Christian living sometimes means suffering—and we should set our minds to suffer gracefully as a testimony to a world that attempts to avoid suffering at all costs. We may suffer persecution from unbelievers—or even other believers. We may suffer in our flesh as we take up our cross and follow Him. We may suffer in our souls as we learn to grow in faith. At the least, we know that if we live a godly in Christ Jesus we will suffer persecution (2 Timothy 3:12).

I don't know about you. But I would rather suffer than fail to please God. If I have to suffer, and it seems that some measure of suffering is unavoidable in this earthly tent, then I'd rather do it for the right reasons than the wrong reasons. Consider the words of Peter, "For what glory is it, if, when ye be buffeted for your faults, ye shall take it patiently? but if, when ye do well, and suffer for it, ye take it patiently, this is acceptable with God" (1 Peter 2:20). If we suffer gracefully for doing the will of God, God will more than make it up to us. We must continue to trust Him even if we face Job-like experiences. Of course, the truth is that most of us will never suffer like Job did. Again, it's a matter of perspective.

It's been said, "Most people are quite happy to suffer in silence, if they are sure everybody knows they are doing it." That used to be my philosophy. I didn't want to ruin my "good confession" by complaining about the flu bug, the sprained ankle, or the unjust client I was "suffering with." But you know as well as I do that we can display our suffering without opening our mouths and saying a word. Do you remember what the Pharisees did when they fasted?

> "Whenever you fast, do not put on a gloomy face as the hypocrites do, for they neglect their appearance so that they will be noticed by men when they are fasting."
>
> —Matthew 6:16 (NASB)

When I wasn't well, I might not have opened my mouth and told anybody—but many times you could tell by the look on my face. A friend of mine displayed her suffering in a different way. She wouldn't tell you what was going on and why she had an "excuse" to behave badly. She would just hint, "You have no idea how much I'm dealing with right now! I'm not even going to speak it!" Well, in her mind, this statement gave her to a license to behave in a less-than-Christ-like manner—and to overlook it by offering a blanket excuse about some unnamed trial. That's not suffering gracefully. Suffering gracefully is when we bear up under a thing and keep blessing people with a smile on our face. Suffering gracefully is when we feel like our guts are being torn out, yet we continue executing our responsibilities without making others around us feel like they are walking on eggshells. Suffering gracefully is having the maturity to understand that "this too shall pass" and making efforts to ensure you are learning every lesson you can through the experience.

American Writer Elbert Hubbard once said, "If you suffer, thank God!—it's a sure sign that you are alive." The New Testament has plenty to say about suffering and how to respond to it. If we are going to live victorious Christian lives—lives that glorify God—we need to learn how to suffer gracefully. I call it suffering in an attitude of victory.

A Victorious Response to Suffering

What does suffering in an attitude of victory look like? Christ and Paul are two good examples. Christ suffered for us, leaving us an example, that we should follow His steps (1 Peter 2:21). And Paul was willing to suffer all things rather than hinder the Gospel of Christ (1 Corinthians 9:12).

Paul wanted to know Jesus, and the power of His resurrection, and the fellowship of His sufferings, being made conformable unto his death (Philippians 3:10). Paul wasn't afraid to suffer. Can we say the same? British-American Writer Lesley Hazelton sums it up this way: "Suffering, once accepted, loses its edge, for the terror of it lessens, and what remains is generally far more manageable than we had imagined." Paul accepted his lot of suffering. In fact, he knew how much he would suffer when he responded to his calling.

> "But the Lord said to [Ananias], Go, for this man is a chosen instrument of Mine to bear My name before the Gentiles and kings and the descendants of Israel; For I will make clear to him how much he will be afflicted and must endure and suffer for My name's sake."

> —Acts 9:15-16

Paul chose suffering, but he also chose to rejoice in his suffering. When we suffer, we too are supposed to rejoice. The notion of rejoicing in the face of suffering sort of makes your natural mind go tilt. But if we are going to be doers of the Word, let's not leave out this part and deceive ourselves. Rejoicing is not a suggestion. It's a command—and one that's for our own good because rejoicing in the midst of the suffering comforts our soul, strengthens our faith, and confuses the enemy.

When you suffer shame for standing up for the name of Christ, rejoice that you were counted worthy to suffer that shame (Acts 5:41). I mean literally, physically praise God and leap for joy! When you suffer insults and persecution and people falsely say evil things about you for Christ's sake, rejoice and be exceeding glad because your reward in heaven is great (Matthew 5:11-12). If we rejoice at all times, we demonstrate a victorious Christian life that doesn't rely on outward circumstances for its joy. Rejoice! The world is watching—and so is Jesus.

The bottom line: When we suffer for righteousness' sake, we're actually supposed to be happy about it (1 Peter 3:14). We are supposed to be happy in knowing that the God of all grace, who has called us unto His eternal glory by Christ Jesus, after we have suffered a while, will mature us, establish us, strengthen us, and settle us (1 Peter 5:10). That's something to rejoice about!

God is Your Vindicator

Don't try to take vindication into your own hands. When Jesus suffered, He didn't make threats. He committed Himself to the Righteous Judge (1 Peter 2:23). When you suffer in any way, remember who you have believed—Jesus, the Son of God—and realize that He is able to keep that which you have committed to Him (2 Timothy 1:12).

We live in a society today where the goal seems to be alleviating suffering. When we have a headache, we don't just take aspirin. We don't even settle for "extra strength" aspirin. The drug store shelves are now lined with "maximum strength" pain reliever. I'm not a glutton for suffering. No one likes it. But there are times when experiencing suffering seems necessary in order to come up to another level. When suffering is not necessary—when children are going hungry in Third World nations, for example—we should work to alleviate that suffering. But when suffering is necessary in order to refine our character, we should not try to run from it. There's really nowhere to run. I believe that by trying to escape suffering, we are only prolonging our suffering. The suffering I am speaking of is really just suffering to crucify our flesh.

I speak from experience. I remember a time in my walk when I tried to avoid suffering like the proverbial plague. I expertly maneuvered around difficult meetings, unpleasant people, or undesirable situations rather than going through with trust in God.

Then the Holy Spirit told me this: "Stop trying to get out of things." It's always a good idea to take the Holy Spirit's advice. And I would soon have an opportunity.

Here's how it happened. I was set up. Publicly painted in a light that was not only inaccurate—it was devil-inspired. I knew I was taking the unfair fall for something I hadn't done. I knew I was about to be lambasted publicly in a way that was not only inappropriate but also based on completely erroneous information. How did I know? The Holy Spirit told me ahead of time.

I had two choices. I could have skipped the public lambasting and gone home to spend a quiet afternoon with my daughter. Or I could go into the public lambasting and willingly suffer the angry and unfair treatment. I decided to "stop trying to get out of things." I went to the meeting, along with about 30 others, where I was made a public example. Even though the truth came out later, no apology was offered me, either private or public. Needless to say, this was an uncomfortable meeting for me.

But I was able to suffer through it knowing I was suffering for something I had done right rather than something I had done wrong. I was able to see the true colors of some people, not only by the angry outburst but also by their decision not to apologize or even acknowledge the truth once the truth came out and, moreover, to begin treating me worse than ever.

I suffered persecution in that meeting. But the glory of the Lord was upon me. I learned plenty about humility, how to respond gracefully to a public attack, and what true leadership is about.

Indeed, that meeting was a major turning point in my life and ministry. Had I not been willing to suffer being publicly shamed for something I didn't do, I would not have been able to move forward in His plan for my life. Perhaps ironically, God used that persecution as an instrument to release me from bondage. If you are suffering unfair treatment, remember that God is your Vindicator. In the end, He always vindicates. Winston Churchill said, "Mountaintops inspire leaders but valleys mature them." Don't try to get out of your valley prematurely. Wait on God.

If you are suffering, remember this: "There hath no temptation taken you but such as is common to man: but God is faithful, who will not suffer you to be tempted above that ye are able; but will with the temptation also make a way to escape, that ye may be able to bear it" (1 Corinthians 10:13).

At the end of the day, also remember what Paul said, "I reckon that the sufferings of this present time are not worthy to be compared with the glory which shall be revealed in us" (Romans 8:18). That's not the only promise. Here's another: "If we suffer, we shall also reign with him" (2 Timothy 2:12). Discipline yourself to be a doer of the Word, and rejoice in your trials. Although we receive many rewards in this lifetime, many others are awaiting us in heaven. Our citizenship is in heaven. There's no suffering there. You can do this!

Breakthrough Exercise:
Keys to Self-Discipline

We have faith that moves mountains. Sometimes, though, victorious Christian living means conquering self before we can conquer the mountain. Vince Lombardi once said, "The good Lord gave you a body that can stand most anything. It's your mind you have to convince." Self-discipline starts in the mind. Here are some action steps to developing self-discipline in your life that will even endure life's sufferings:

1. Start small. There may be many areas of your life that demand a new level of discipline. Don't try to change everything at once or you will get overwhelmed and reinforce the belief that you can't change. Pick what seems to be the easiest area of discipline, whether that's getting up an hour earlier to spend more time with the Lord or just washing the dishes right after dinner every night. Once you've conquered one area, move on to the next.

2. Practice self-denial. Learn to say no to yourself. Delayed gratification breeds greater appreciation. Many people wind up in debt or overweight because they didn't practice self-denial. Implement a system of incentives where you reward yourself for reaching goals rather than just doing what you want when you want.

3. The key of finishing. When you start a task, complete it. So many of us have half-completed tasks. This drains your mental energy. Go back and tie up all the loose ends in your life and discipline yourself to finish what you start from now on.

4. Get organized. Make a list every week of what you need to get done, either at your job, on the home front, in your finances or some other area of your life. Next, prioritize your list. Finally, execute your list according to the priorities you've set. No excuses.

CHAPTER 8

Victory Habit #6
Live a Pure Life

*As obedient children, not fashioning yourselves
according to the former lusts in your ignorance:
But as he which hath called you is holy, so be ye
holy in all manner of conversation; Because it is
written, Be ye holy; for I am holy.*

—1 Peter 1:14-16

We've come a long way on our journey to building habits that pave the way to a victorious Christian life. But we're not done yet. The sixth habit of victorious Christian living is purely vital: purity. Without purity, you can't sustain the other habits. If you know the Word and decide not to live a pure life, you aren't holding tightly to the truth and you'll deceive yourself. If you aren't interested in living a pure life, you won't want to stir up the gift, focus on Christ, or discipline yourself, either. Purity is part and parcel of victorious Christian living. We all make mistakes, of course, but we're talking about the motive of the heart to consistently live a pure life.

Consecrating yourself isn't a one-time event. We have to make a habit of keeping ourselves pure. Indeed, Paul told Timothy to get into the habit of living a pure life. He explained that whoever cleanses himself will be a vessel set apart for God's use, fit and ready for good works. Consider Paul's words:

> "Shun youthful lusts and flee from them, and aim at and pursue righteousness (all that is virtuous and good, right living, conformity to the will of God in thought, word and deed; [and aim at and pursue] faith, love, [and] peace (harmony and concord with others) in fellowship with all [Christians], who call upon the Lord out of a pure heart."

> —2 Timothy 2:22 (AMP)

Putting Off the Old Man

Victorious Christian living makes a habit of shunning the old man and all its lusts. Shun is a strong word. It means "to avoid deliberately and especially habitually." So when Paul told Timothy to shun youthful lusts, he meant to make a habit of deliberately staying away from these temptations. That directive works hand in hand with James' Spirit-inspired command to resist the devil and he will flee (4:7). We need to shun circumstances that would put us in a position to resist the devil in the first place. We need to flee before we have the occasion to resist the devil. If we don't flee and we fail to resist, the devil won't flee either. The result can compromise our purity.

I'm a single mother, and the mothers of my teenaged daughter's two best friends are also single. Both of these women are "good people" as we say in the South. I trust them to pick up my daughter from school, to host her at their homes for sleepovers, and to take her about anywhere they'd take their own daughters. It's fair to say that these women are even more over-protective than I am (though my daughter would disagree). They are good people. They are good mothers who instill strong values in their kids.

However, when weekend comes, watch out. They don't live a pure life. They go out to clubs and party all night. I've been invited on many occasions to "go out with the girls." But I politely shun those invitations because I know it would compromise my pure lifestyle. Having done plenty of clubbing, drinking, and smoking as a teenager, why would I want to tempt myself by going to a club? I don't even have any desire to go to a club. The Holy Spirit wouldn't let me get away with it anyway. Those youthful lusts don't even appeal to me, and I am just wise enough to know that even a strong, victorious Christian can get burned if they play with the devil's fire. So you won't find me in the clubs. I deliberately choose to sanctify myself by the grace of God. It's a deliberate choice we all have to make when it comes to any "youthful lust."

Richard Mentor Johnson, the ninth vice president of the United States of America, once said: "Let the professors of Christianity recommend their religion by deeds of benevolence—by Christian meekness—by lives of temperance and holiness."

I am far from perfect, but when it comes to my fellow single mothers, I have chosen to demonstrate a life in pursuit of holiness. And guess who these women come to for advice when they have problems? I have an opportunity to plant seeds for a harvest of salvation. Oh, they see I'm far from perfect. I don't try to act holier than them. But they also see my heart after God.

Some people may think I'm weird because I'd rather stay home and read my Bible than go to the club until all hours of the night. Again, I don't act self-righteous about it. When I get those invitations, I just tell the girls I'm busy and suggest we get together for dinner next week. We all have to make a choice. I choose to do what Paul describes in Romans 12:1-2:

> "I beseech you therefore, brethren, by the mercies of God, that ye present your bodies a living sacrifice, holy, acceptable unto God, which is your reasonable service. And be not conformed to this world: but be ye transformed by the renewing of your mind, that ye may prove what is that good, and acceptable, and perfect, will of God."

Holy, Holy, Holy

I don't know about you, but songs about the holiness of God really touch me. There are entire books on God's holiness, but I want to talk about our progressive holiness in Him. The Bible says, "Be ye holy even as I am holy" (I Peter 1:16).

Sixteenth Century Presbyterian Minister Matthew Henry once said, "No attribute of God is more dreadful to sinners than His holiness." For children of God, His holiness should not breed dread. It should breed a reverential fear and awe of Him. God is holy. God's name is Holy. God's covenant is holy (Luke 1:72). God's angels are holy (Luke 11:13). God's Word is holy (Romans 1:2). We need not dread God's holiness because we are holy in Christ. He has called us into holiness through faith in His beloved Son. Let's take a look at how the Father sees us through the blood of Jesus:

> "May blessing (praise, laudation, and eulogy) be to the God and Father of our Lord Jesus Christ (the Messiah) Who has blessed us in Christ with every spiritual (given by the Holy Spirit) blessing in the heavenly realm!
>
> Even as [in His love] He chose us [actually picked us out for Himself as His own] in Christ before the foundation of the world, that we should be holy (consecrated and set apart for Him) and blameless in His sight, even above reproach, before Him in love."
>
> —Ephesians 1:3-4 (AMP)

> "And you, that were sometime alienated and enemies in your mind by wicked works, yet now hath he reconciled. In the body of his flesh through death, to present you holy

and unblameable and unreproveable
in his sight…"

—Colossians 1:21-23

When Father God looks at us, He sees us as holy
and without blame—because of our faith in His
Son. We are consecrated and set apart for Him.
He made us holy because it pleased Him and was
His kind intent. Victorious Christians meditate on
that truth until the mind is renewed to it. With an
understanding that God has consecrated us for
Himself in His mercy and by His grace and with
His love, we will yearn to be holy even as He is
holy in our daily lives. We will shun youthful
lusts and flee from the ways of the old man.

Consider Paul's words to Timothy in 2 Timothy
1:9 (AMP):

> "[For it is He] Who delivered and
> saved us and called us with a
> calling in itself holy and leading to
> holiness [to a life of consecration, a
> vocation of holiness]; [He did it]
> not because of anything of merit
> that we have done, but because of
> and to further His own purpose and
> grace (unmerited favor) which was
> given us in Christ Jesus before the
> world began [eternal ages ago]."

Grace to Live Holy

It's vital to remember that we aren't holy on our own accord. Our righteousness is as filthy rags (Isaiah 64:6). We can't be holy in and of ourselves. Thirteenth Century German Writer and Theologian Meister Eckhardt said once said something profound:

> "People should not worry as much about what they do but rather about what they are. If they and their ways are good, then their deeds are radiant. If you are righteous, then what you do will also be righteous. We should not think that holiness is based on what we do but rather on what we are, for it is not our works which sanctify us but we who sanctify our works."

We cannot become righteous by our works. But our holiness should spur righteous works. We cannot make ourselves holy, but there is a proper response to God's saving grace. God expects us to present our bodies a living sacrifice in holiness, to renew our minds to His way of thinking, and to love one another.

> "Put on therefore, as the elect of God, holy and beloved, bowels of mercies, kindness, humbleness of

mind, meekness, longsuffering; Forbearing one another, and forgiving one another, if any man have a quarrel against any: even as Christ forgave you, so also do ye."

—Colossians 3:11-13

I can't stress this enough because I've seen too many people wear themselves out trying to achieve holiness. In fact, I've done it myself. Listen, even as we pursue purity and holiness— even as we yield our members servants of righteousness unto holiness—we need to be careful not to pursue holiness in our own strength. Again, our righteousness is like filthy rags. There's nothing holy in us apart from Him. If we want to bear fruit unto holiness, we need to rely on the grace of God. We need to simply get into agreement with Him and use our faith as a channel to receive His power to live a pure and holy life. It's His will, and He's willing to help us. That's Good News!

It takes grace to cleanse ourselves from all filthiness of the flesh and spirit, perfecting holiness in the fear of God (2 Corinthians 7:1). It takes grace to put on the new man, which after God is created in righteousness and true holiness (Ephesians 4:24). The good news is the grace, or power of the Holy Spirit, is available to anyone who will believe God for it and yield to it. Victorious Christian living relies on the grace of God to live a holy life. Remember the words of Mother Theresa: "True holiness consists of doing God's will with a smile."

Breakthrough Exercise: Pursue Holiness

Oswald Chambers, author of the classic daily devotional "My Utmost for His Highest," once said, "Holiness, not happiness, is the chief end of man." Let's put our faith in action to live a holy life. Here are some steps that will help you.

1. Set your heart to follow holiness. Hebrews 12:14 says, "Follow peace with all men, and holiness, without which no man shall see the Lord." What does it mean to follow holiness? It means to pursue holiness wholeheartedly. Meditate on Scriptures about the holiness of God. Confess that you are holy even as He is holy. Repent of any known sin and determine in your heart to live a consecrated life. Get in hot pursuit of holiness!

2. Cut off unholy influences. You may have unholy influences in your life right now. If you do, cut them off. That may mean not talking to certain people any longer, or it may just mean not participating in the same activities with them, whether it be going to the club or gossiping.

Jesus said, "And if thy hand offend thee, cut it off: it is better for thee to enter into life maimed, than having two hands to go into hell, into the fire that never shall be quenched: Where their worm dieth not, and the fire is not quenched. And if thy foot offend thee, cut it off: it is better for thee to enter halt into life, than having two feet to be cast into hell, into the fire that never shall be quenched: Where their worm dieth not, and the fire is not quenched. And if thine eye offend thee, pluck it out: it is better for thee to enter into the kingdom of God with one eye, than having two eyes to be cast into hell fire: Where their worm dieth not, and the fire is not quenched" (Mark 9:43-48).

CHAPTER 8

Victory Habit #7
Pour Your Life into Others

Pass on what you heard from me—the whole congregation saying Amen!—to reliable leaders who are competent to teach others.

—2 Timothy 2:2

Paul knew that spreading the unadulterated Gospel to the nations depended on inspiring and equipping others with the truth in which he walked. But Paul also knew that Timothy couldn't fulfill his destiny in his own strength— none of us can. That's why Paul told Timothy to be strong in the grace that is found only in Christ Jesus as he set out to raise up others in ministry (2 Timothy 2:1). Paul was calling Timothy to a higher level of leadership.

> "The [instructions] which you have heard from me along with many witnesses, transmit and entrust [as a deposit] to reliable and faithful men who will be competent and qualified to teach others also."

—2 Timothy 2:2 (AMP)

Victorious Christian living is not all about you. This lifestyle demands investing in others so they, too, can live victoriously and fulfill their destiny. Of course, you can't invest your life in anyone and everyone. There simply aren't enough hours in the day. You need wisdom to decide whom to mentor.

Notice that Paul qualified his instruction to Timothy. He told him to choose "reliable and faithful men." Victorious Christian living takes into account the need to redeem the time by pouring into those who are pursuing God with their whole hearts. We should pray for all saints, but part of redeeming the time is understanding who isn't yet ready to be mentored—or who God hasn't called us to mentor—as well as those we are called to raise up.

The Body of Christ is suffering from a lack of spiritual mentors. This must not be so. I've heard "mentor" defined as "someone whose hindsight can become your foresight." Imagine if each generation had to start from scratch, digging out revelation from the Word of God that believers freely walked in centuries ago. Thank God for books and CDs that have recorded the revelations and outpourings of the past. We can build on the revelation our spiritual forefathers deposited into the Body of Christ. But we also need to actively impart present-day truth to those around us. We need to keep the torch of revelation burning, and willingly pass it to those coming up behind us. Winston Churchill once said, "We make a living by what we get. We make a life by what we give." Victorious Christian living isn't threatened by another's success; it's pouring our your life so others can take the Gospel even farther than you.

An unknown wise man once said, "A lot of people have gone further than they thought they could because someone else thought they could." We all need someone to believe in us. Spiritual mentors have never been more vital than they are in this hour.

Christians need to walk in victory so they can pull others up from the miry clay in which the devil has trapped them. But without more mature Christians willing to get their hands a little dirty through spiritual mentorship, much of the Body will remain in diapers. Again, spiritual mentors have never been more vital than they are in this hour. I call this cry for spiritual mentors the Malachi Mandate.

The Malachi Mandate

There's plenty of reflection among Christians about the spirit of Elijah. Doubtless, this Old Testament mouthpiece offers copious character traits that his New Testament counterparts would do well to model. However, for all the accurate prophetic decrees and miraculous moments that characterized Elijah's ministry, it is his spiritual mentorship that is perhaps most needed in the Body of Christ today.

With companies of young prophets rising up and armies of prophetic believers awakening to establish the Kingdom of God throughout all the earth, spiritual guidance is vital to a stable Church that the world will look to for answers.

Governments and other secular leaders won't bow their ears to the utterances of super spiritual fruits, emotional flakes and hypocritical nuts. The governing church demands unwavering voices that refuse to compromise in the face of opposition, yet with a wisdom and grace that persuades even the hardest heart's that God's will is the only way.

The full manifestation of the sons of God depends on spiritual fathers, mothers and mentors who will invest time and energy into others. So as we consider Elijah and his miraculous ministry let us also remember this powerful prophet's role in shaping the life and ministry of young Elisha, who went on to do far greater things than his spiritual mentor.

Understanding Spiritual Fathers

Some of the characteristics of a spiritual father are protection, guidance, instruction, correction, exhortation, encouragement and inspiration. Paul the apostle is a good example of a spiritual father. You could sense the love he had for those he served.

Let's be clear: You don't have to be an apostle, prophet, evangelist, pastor or teacher to be a spiritual father, mother or mentor. You just need to be willing to engage in a relational dynamic that will prepare the Church for its Bridegroom. That means giving of yourself—not so you can get something in return, but so you can have the pleasure of seeing another matured and released to exercise their unique gifts for the glory of God.

We are beginning to see the manifestation of the Malachi mandate that proclaims: "He shall turn the heart of the fathers to the children, and the heart of the children to their fathers..." (Malachi 4:6) But we have a way to go as of the time of this writing.

Many church leaders mourn the dearth of spiritual fathers in the Body of Christ today. I believe one reason for the scarcity of spiritual mentors is the lack of a widespread mentoring model in former generations. Many of today's local church leaders tell me they were not mentored themselves, and subsequently do not know how to mentor others.

Of course, the concept of spiritual fatherhood is not new. Dr. Lester Sumrall raised up three strong spiritual sons. Sumrall passed away in 1996, but his ministry lives on, in part, through what he imparted to Rod Parsley, Ulf Ekman and Billy Joe Daugherty. Sumrall was known as a "pastor of pastors." Sumrall, himself, was tutored by British evangelist Howard Carter and blessed by Smith Wigglesworth.

Recognizing False Spiritual Fathers

Sumrall was a true spiritual father—and you can still see the fruit of his mentorship glorifying God today. But there are also what I'll call false spiritual fathers.

Earlier, I mentioned some of the characteristics of a spiritual father. These include protection, guidance, instruction, correction, exhortation, encouragement, and inspiration. Spiritual fathers should protect you from what you can't see in your inexperience or immaturity by sharing practical wisdom. Spiritual fathers should offer guidance and instruction in how to walk out the Word in your life. Spiritual fathers should exhort you, encourage you, and inspire you to seek and follow God's will for your life. All of this demands relationship.

Spiritual fathers will also bring correction, which is important to growing in God. God sometimes chastens us Himself, and sometimes uses leaders to chasten us. Nobody likes that part of spiritual mentorship, but it is sometimes necessary. The writer of Hebrews said, "No discipline seems pleasant at the time, but painful. Later on, however, it produces a harvest of righteousness and peace for those who have been trained by it" (Hebrews 12:11).

Correction can be a good thing. But when spiritual mentoring relationships become centered on constant berating without much protection, guidance, instruction, exhortation, encouragement and inspiration, the relationship rapidly grows unhealthy. The spirit in which the correction comes is vital. God is slow to anger, full of grace and rich in mercy (Psalm 145:8). As a spiritual mentor, you should model that attitude.

Unfortunately, as the spiritual fathering movement has gained momentum some tares have sprung up with the wheat. Those tares manifest as control, fear and intimidation over spiritual sons and daughters. I'm not going to do an expose on this topic here. Suffice it to say that just as there are false apostle and false prophets, there can be false spiritual mentors, those who are more concerned about what you can do for them than what they can do for you. They are users and abusers. You'll know them by their fruit. What fruit? Look for spiritual mentors who display the Sermon on the Mount lifestyle.

Recognizing True Spiritual Fathers

So what does a true spiritual father look like? I mentioned a few characteristics earlier in this chapter. But let's look at how Scripture bears it out—not with mere descriptive buzzwords but in clear-cut actions that demonstrate how spiritual fathers responded to their spiritual children.

Paul's heartfelt care and concern for his spiritual sons leaps from the pages of his epistles. True spiritual fathers and mothers have true relationships with their spiritual children—and those relationships are rooted in the love of Christ. Paul trained Timothy, not to forward Paul's ministry but to forward the Kingdom.

Paul repeatedly spoke grace, mercy and peace over Timothy's life, despite his character flaws (1 Timothy 1:2; 2 Timothy 1:2). Paul encouraged Timothy when he was afraid (2 Timothy 1:7). Paul shared his heart and his wisdom with Timothy so he could be a more effective minister of the Gospel (2 Timothy). Paul even cared about Timothy's stomach problems (1 Timothy 5:23). Paul prayed for Timothy constantly, rather than just demanding Timothy's service to him (2 Timothy 1:3-7). Paul was grateful to have Timothy in his life and he treated Timothy with respect.

Consider the spiritual dynamic between Paul and Timothy: "Every time I say your name in prayer—which is practically all the time—I thank

God for you, the God I worship with my whole life in the tradition of my ancestors. I miss you a lot, especially when I remember that last tearful good-bye, and I look forward to a joy-packed reunion" (2 Timothy 1:3-4 Message).

This is a true spiritual father. You can't rent a spiritual father. Once again, spiritual mentoring demands relationship. True spiritual accountability, which is vital in this hour, comes out of true, balanced, healthy relationships where the spiritual mentors have the best interests of their spiritual mentees at heart, even if that means releasing them into what God has for them next.

A spiritual father loves at all times. When correction must come, it comes out of a spirit of love rather than a spirit of fear, control, intimidation, manipulation, or condemnation. Think about it for a minute. Even with all the problems in the Corinthian church—and there were many, including divisions, carnality, immorality, fornication, abusing the Lord's supper, a lack of love, disorder, and wrong teachings about the resurrection of the dead—the Apostle Paul said this: "I have the highest confidence in you, and I take great pride in you. You have greatly encouraged me and made me happy despite all our troubles" (2 Corinthians 7:4). That's the heart of a true spiritual father.

Remember it was Paul, a strong model of a spiritual father, who the Holy Spirit used to offer us a revelation of what love in action looks like. Although every one has bad days and goes through trials, 1 Corinthians 13:4 reveals how those who deem themselves spiritual fathers, mothers and mentors should behave toward those under their care:

Love is patient and kind.
Love is not jealous or boastful or proud or rude.
Love does not demand its own way.
Love is not irritable.
Love keeps no record of being wronged.
Love does not rejoice about injustice.
Love rejoices whenever the truth wins out.
Love never gives up.
Love never loses faith.
Love is always hopeful.
Love endures through every circumstance.

Breakthrough Exercise:

Find (and Be) a Mentor

Everyone needs a mentor and everyone needs to be mentored. None of us has arrived and there is always more to learn. The depth of the Word of God is endless, and we can learn from the mistakes of others so we don't have to walk through the same places.

Here are some things you can do in the spirit of 2 Timothy 2:2:

1. Look for someone to mentor. When you see new believers come into your congregation, extend the right hand of fellowship, spend a little time getting to know them. If God leads you to take someone under your wing, be obedient.

2. Look for someone to mentor you. Look for people who are more mature in the Lord than you; people who are willing to share their experiences, advice, and sound teachings with you. Understanding that you probably won't be best friends with your pastor or his wife, find opportunities to glean from your elders so you can be more effective in your Christian walk.

CHAPTER 9

The Eighth Habit:
Build a Relationship
with the Holy Spirit

Guard the good deposit that was entrusted to you—guard it with the help of the Holy Spirit who lives in us.

—2 Timothy 1:14 (NIV)

Throughout this book, we've been discussing Scriptural habits of victorious Christian living. If you paid attention, you noticed that the Holy Spirit is central to living a victorious life. We need the grace of God. Apart from the Holy Spirit, we can do nothing. Indeed, 17th Century British Poet William Blake put it best when he said, "I myself do nothing. The Holy Spirit accomplishes all through me."

And so there is an eighth habit, one that

empowers you to establish and maintain all the others: Building a relationship with the Holy Spirit. What do I mean when I say building a relationship with the Holy Spirit? I mean having a binding connection with Him—and being aware of that binding connection—at all times. The Holy Spirit is always with us, and He longs to help us live a victorious Christian life.

The Holy Spirit is my best friend on earth. He is the most precious person in the world. He counsels me when I need wisdom. He helps me when I face problems. He teaches me the Word of God. He prays for me when I don't know how. He pleads my case with Father God. He strengthens my spirit. He helps me resist the devil. He's always by my side. He gave me beauty for ashes, the oil of joy for mourning. Whether you know the Holy Spirit in those ways, or just want to build a stronger relationship with Him, my prayer is that this chapter will inspire you to draw nigh to the Spirit of Grace who empowers you to live a victorious Christian life. Yes, He is the Spirit of Grace, the Spirit of Truth, and the Spirit of Liberty. He is the Spirit of the Lord. He wants to counsel you, help you, teach you, pray for you, strengthen you, and give you beauty for ashes.

Who is the Holy Spirit?

Many of you know Jesus and many of you know the Father, but far fewer know the Holy Spirit or have a relationship with Him in their daily lives. Before we can build a deep relationship with the Holy Spirit, we need a clear understanding of who He is—and who He is not.

The Holy Spirit is the third person of the Trinity. The Holy Spirit is just as much God as the Father and the Son are God. He is eternal (Hebrews 9:14). He was present with God at the creation of the world (Genesis 1:2). He is omnipresent (Psalms 139:7-10). He is omniscient (1 Corinthians 1:20-11). He is omnipotent (Psalms 104:30). The Holy Spirit is not a mist, not a cloud, not a strange feeling. And He has feelings just like you and me. He is sensitive and compassionate. You can grieve the Holy Spirit (Ephesians 4:20). He has a will (1 Corinthians 12:11). He has a personality characterized by love (Romans 15:30), goodness, patience, joy, peace, kindness, faithfulness, gentleness, and self-control (Galatians 5:22-23), holiness (Romans 1:4), truth (John 16:13), grace (Hebrews 10:29), and comfort (John 15:26).

The Holy Spirit is not only powerful and mighty, He is the power of God. He is the change agent. He is God in action on the earth. He longs to be an active part of your life. And He takes pleasure in sharing His power, His grace, His counsel. But He's a Gentleman and He won't force His fellowship on you. You have to want Him. He's waiting.

The Holy Spirit Helps Us

If you haven't pressed in to build a deep relationship with the Holy Spirit, it's probably because you haven't been taught how integral He is to living a victorious Christian life. Remember Blake's comments: "I myself do nothing. The Holy Spirit accomplishes all through me."

Without the Holy Spirit's help, we can't forgive those who hurt us. Without the Holy Spirit's help, we can't walk in love, for the love of God is shed abroad in our hearts by the Holy Ghost (Romans 5:5). Without the Holy Ghost, we can't pray as we ought (Romans 8:26). Without the Holy Spirit, we can't prophesy (2 Peter 1:21). Without the Holy Spirit, we can't be effective witnesses (John 15:26). Without the Holy Spirit, we can't gain victory over our flesh (Romans 8:4, 13).

Thank God Jesus sent the Holy Spirit to help us. When Jesus foretold the coming of the Spirit, He called Him "another Comforter." The Amplified version of the Bible stretches that out and calls the Holy Spirit, Comforter Counselor, Helper, Intercessor, Advocate, Strengthener, and Standby (John 14:26 AMP). When you consider the many wonderful roles the Holy Spirit plays in our lives—or wants to play if we'll let Him—it's jaw dropping. The Holy Spirit gives us life (Romans 8:11). The Holy Spirit gives us hope (Romans 15:13). The Holy Spirit gives us joy (Romans 14:17). The Holy Spirit gives us skills (Exodus

31:2-5). The Holy Spirit gives us physical strength (Judges 14:6) and spiritual strength (Ephesians 3:16). The Holy Spirit gives us boldness (Acts 1:8). The Holy Spirit gives us revelation (Ephesians 1:16).

I could go on and on and on. Many volumes have been written on the Holy Spirit. I would recommend "The Greatest Power in the World" by Kathryn Kuhlman and "Holy Spirit Revelation & Revolution" by Reinhard Bonnke as good books to start with.

The Holy Spirit really is your Helper. He'll help you establish the good habits—and break the bad ones—that lead to victorious Christian living. You have a part to play, but you can't accomplish your part without the Holy Spirit. 20th Century Evangelist Aimee Semple McPherson offers wisdom that helps us separate our part from His part: "What is my task? First of all, my task is to be pleasing to Christ. To be empty of self and be filled with Himself. To be filled with the Holy Spirit; to be led by the Holy Spirit." It's just that simple.

Practice the Presence of God

How do you get closer to the Holy Ghost? The best way I know is to practice the presence of God. See, the Holy Spirit is with you and in you. It's a guarantee from Jesus:

"And I will pray the Father, and he shall give you another Comforter, that he may abide with you for ever; Even the Spirit of truth; whom the world cannot receive, because it seeth him not, neither knoweth him: but ye know him; for he dwelleth with you, and shall be in you."

—John 14:16-17

The Father has given us the gift of the Holy Spirit. But again, He is a Gentleman. He is not going to force His will on your life any more than the Father forces His will on your life or Jesus forces His will on your life. He is standing by. He is waiting for you to ask Him for help. He is waiting for you to ask Him for counsel. He is waiting for you to ask Him for comfort. He is waiting for you to ask Him for grace. He is waiting for you to fellowship with Him so He can lead you into truth that will set you free. He is waiting for you to spend time in His presence so that He can refresh you. He is waiting for you to get into the Word so He can reveal Scriptures to you. He is waiting.

Walk, Think, Talk

So how do you practice the presence of God? Brother Lawrence wrote a classic book on the topic. I'd highly recommend picking it up. But for our purposes, practicing the presence of God starts with being God-inside conscious instead of sin conscious.

Practically speaking, we need to walk as in the presence of God. Would you still go to all the same places if you had a strong realization that God was literally there in your presence? Selah.

We also need to think as in the presence of God. What if your thoughts were made public to the world? Most of us wouldn't like our co-workers to hear what rolls around in our heads. Well, our thoughts are public to God. So think about what you're thinking about and get rid of the stinking thinking. Cast down imaginations, and every high thing that exalts itself against the knowledge of God, and bring into captivity every thought to the obedience of Christ (2 Corinthians 10:5).

I'm not even suggesting that you are thinking utterly worldly thoughts. But what about the thoughts of self-defeat and self-doubt that you meditate on? We all need to continually renew our minds with the Word of God. The Holy Spirit even helps us do that.

Finally, we need to talk as in the presence of God. Again, the Holy Spirit hears our every word. He knows what we are going to say before we say it—for better or worse—and He loves us anyway. But He doesn't always love what we say. What's more, whereas our thoughts are private from the world's perspective, what we say is often public, even if it's only within earshot of those closest to us.

What we say can hurt the faith—and the feelings—of others. Gossip, complaining and backbiting, for example, grieve the Holy Spirit and could tempt others to engage in these sinful activities. Don't let what you say cause others to stumble. The Apostle Paul put it this way, "Let no corrupt communication proceed out of your mouth, but that which is good to the use of edifying, that it may minister grace unto the hearers" (Ephesians 4:29).

Remember this: Whatever is not of faith is sin. The Holy Spirit convicts us of sin (John 16:8-11). That's good news, because when we're walking, thinking, and talking in ways that don't line up with the Word of God, the Holy Spirit will gently nudge us so we can stop, repent, and receive forgiveness. The key is being sensitive to Him. Building a deeper relationship with the Holy Spirit opens the door to the next glory in our transformation into Christ's image:

> "Now the Lord is that Spirit: and
> where the Spirit of the Lord is,

there is liberty. But we all, with unveiled face beholding as in a mirror the glory of the Lord, are being transformed into the same image from glory to glory, just as from the Lord, the Spirit."

—2 Corinthians 3:17-18

With all that said, let's keep the main thing the main thing. Victorious Christian living isn't all about us. It's not just about us having peace and joy and wisdom and revelation. It's about fulfilling the Great Commission. I like the way American author Jeffrey Bryant said it:

"Our deepest calling is not to grow in our knowledge of God. It is to make disciples. Our knowledge will grow—the Holy Spirit, Jesus promised, will guide us into all truth. But that's not our calling, it is His. Our calling is to prepare the world for Christ's return. The world is not ready yet. And so, we go about introducing a dying world to the Savior of Life. Anything we do toward our own growth must be toward that end."

The Baptism of the Holy Spirit

If you are born again, the Holy Spirit is living in your spirit. But there is yet more. There is the baptism of the Holy Spirit. The Bible teaches there is an experience beyond the new birth where we receive an infilling of the Holy Spirit.

When I first got born again, I was taught that praying in tongues was a demonic manifestation. Maybe you've been taught that, too. But there's plenty of evidence in Scripture that tongues is a supernatural prayer language. Think about it. The devil wants nothing more than to keep us from being filled with the Holy Spirit because this infilling enables us to walk in a power in which there is no defeat. With the power of the God, the name of Christ, and the blood of the Lamb, you are unstoppable as you pursue His will. So let's take a look some Scriptures relating to the baptism of the Holy Spirit.

After His resurrection, Jesus told the disciples that, "Ye shall be baptized with the Holy Ghost not many days hence" (Acts 1:5). Jesus also told them, "Ye shall receive power, after that the Holy Ghost is come upon you" (Acts 1:8). Then we see Jesus' promise come to pass on the Day of Pentecost:

> "And when the day of Pentecost was fully come, they were all with

one accord in one place. And suddenly there came a sound from heaven as of a rushing mighty wind, and it filled all the house where they were sitting. And there appeared unto them cloven tongues like as of fire, and it sat upon each of them. And they were all filled with the Holy Ghost, and began to speak with other tongues, as the Spirit gave them utterance."

—Acts 2:1-4

This is clearly a separate experience than receiving the Holy Spirit in our spirits as part of the new birth. And it's vital to victorious Christian living. So vital in fact that when Paul met up with born-again believers, he was quick to ask them if they were filled with the Spirit of God:

"And it came to pass, that, while Apollos was at Corinth, Paul having passed through the upper coasts came to Ephesus: and finding certain disciples, He said unto them, 'Have ye received the Holy Ghost since ye believed?' And they said unto him, 'We have not so much as heard whether there be any Holy Ghost.'

And he said unto them, 'Unto what then were ye baptized?' And they said, 'Unto John's baptism.' Then said Paul, 'John verily baptized with the baptism of repentance, saying unto the people, that they should believe on him which should come after him, that is, on Christ Jesus.'

When they heard this, they were baptized in the name of the Lord Jesus. And when Paul had laid his hands upon them, the Holy Ghost came on them; and they spake with tongues, and prophesied."

—Acts 19:1-6

When you receive the baptism of the Holy Spirit, it will empower you to live a victorious Christian life for the glory of God. Yes, you still have your part to play—yielding to the work of the Holy Spirit. But you have an advantage that the world doesn't have.

Receiving the Holy Spirit

How can you receive the Holy Spirit? You first have to believe that the Holy Spirit is a gift from God. So let's look at what Jesus said as recorded in John 16:7:

> "I tell you the truth; It is expedient for you that I go away: for if I go not away, the Comforter will not come unto you; but if I depart, I will send him unto you."

Did Jesus ever tell a lie? Of course not. Is He waiting for you to manifest perfect behavior before you can be filled with the Holy Spirit? Absolutely not! He wants to fill you with the Holy Spirit so you can be perfected, not because you already are. Much like when you got saved, God didn't expect you to come to His throne all cleaned up to ask forgiveness. He knew you were a mess. He wanted you to come to His throne to find mercy and receive grace to clean up your mess. Now, He wants to fill you with His Spirit so you can walk in His grace, which offers power to overcome any sinful habit.

Jesus said, "If ye then, being evil, know how to give good gifts unto your children: how much more shall your heavenly Father give the Holy Spirit to them that ask him?" (Luke 11:13) If you want to become white hot with passion for the Lord, if you need a spark, if you need to rekindle that love, ask the Lord to fill you to overflowing with His Holy Spirit. Why not pray right now before you close the pages on this book?

Pray with me:

> *Father God, I come to you in the name of Jesus. I thank you that you sent your only begotten Son to save me and I thank you that you desire to fill me with your Holy Spirit. Jesus said, "How much more shall your heavenly Father give the Holy Spirit to those who ask Him."*

> *Right now, I ask you in the name of Jesus to fill me with your Holy Spirit. I receive the indwelling of your Spirit right now and I confess by faith that I am Spirit-filled. I thank you that You have given me a prayer language to communicate with you and I yield my tongue to your Spirit right now. I expect to speak in tongues as the Spirit gives me utterance. I thank you and praise you. Amen!*

Breakthrough Exercise:
Relationship Building 101

It's time to reexamine our relationship with the Holy Ghost. Do you know the Holy Ghost? Do you really know Him? Do you know what delights Him? What grieves Him? Building a relationship with the Holy Spirit doesn't have to be a mysterious endeavor. Here are a few primary relationship-building skills that you can apply.

1. Be committed. Commitment is fundamental to any relationship. Relationships demand a time investment. Be committed to spending time with the Holy Spirit so you can get to know Him better. Study Scriptures about the Holy Spirit, and be committed to improving your relationship with him day by day.

2. Have a listening ear. We have a tendency to talk, talk, talk. If you want to build a closer relationship with the Holy Spirit, let Him get a word in edgewise. Talk to Him, but listen, listen, listen when He talks to you. And do what He says. He's got your best interest at heart.

3. Respect Him. Respect is a cornerstone of any healthy relationship. How much more so with God? Respect His feelings. Respect His leading. Respect His people. Have a reverential fear of the Holy Spirit just as you would the Father. Remember, the Holy Spirit is just as much God as Jesus and the Father.

4. Trust Him. You can't build a relationship without trust. If you can't trust the Holy Spirit, who can you trust? Trust Him. Be open and honest with Him. He already knows everything about you—and He loves you.

CHAPTER 10

Good, Bad and Godly Habits

*All of you, slave and free both, were once held
hostage in a sinful society. Then a huge sum was
paid out for your ransom. So please don't, out of
old habit, slip back into being or doing what
everyone else tells you.*

—1 Corinthians 7:23 (The Message)

Habits. We all have them. Some are good, some
are bad—and some are godly. We all want to
establish godly habits, or, you might say, habits
that glorify God. But it's not enough to know
what we need to do. We also need to know how
to go about doing it.

Although everything is dependent on the grace of
God, we do have a role to play in rooting out,
pulling down, destroying, and throwing down our

bad habits as we set out to build and plant godly ones.

So as we close our study on the *7 Habits of Victorious Christian Living*, I want to spend a few more minutes with you getting bottom line practical about how to break unwanted habits and establish godly ones—again, all by the grace of God.

Let me give you some encouragement right up front, from the lips of motivational speaker Jim Rhon, "You don't have to change that much for it to make a great deal of difference. A few simple disciplines can have a major impact on how your life works out in the next 90 days, let alone in the next 12 months or the next three years."

The What and How of Habits

First, let's look at what a habit is and how it is formed. Merriam-Webster defines a habit as a "manner of conducting oneself." Another definition is "the prevailing disposition or character of a person's thoughts and feelings: mental makeup." Yet another definition is, "a behavior pattern acquired by frequent repetition or physiologic exposure that shows itself in regularity or increased facility of performance: an acquired mode of behavior that has become nearly or completely involuntary."

Strong words. The good news is, as born-again believers we have the nature of Christ. Those old bad habits are remnants of our old nature. We can crucify those old, bad habits and replace them with new, good habits. It all starts in our thought life. You may be familiar with this saying:

> "Watch your thoughts, for they become words. Watch your words, for they become actions. Watch your actions, for they become habits. Watch your habits, for they become character. Watch your character, for it becomes your destiny."

Our destiny is in Christ, but without godly thoughts, godly words, godly actions, godly habits, and godly character, we may never fully reach our full potential in Him. Before we venture into breaking bad habits and forming new ones, let's look at what the Bible has to say about habits.

Bad, Ugly Habits

Habits—good, bad and godly—are a running theme throughout the Bible. God has taken the time to offer His wisdom on habits. Let's do a quick study and glean from that wisdom as we set out to develop godly habits.

First, the bad. Inspired by the Spirit of God, Solomon made clear that, "Slack habits and sloppy work are as bad as vandalism" (Proverbs 18:9). A slack hand is not compatible with the spirit of excellence that brings glory to God. We need to yank the slack out of our hands—and our habits—and rely on the Holy Spirit to empower us to approach everything in life as unto the Lord (Colossians 3:23). When we do everything as unto the Lord, we'll do everything in a spirit of excellence.

Worse than slack habits are evil habits. In the Book of Acts, Simon the Sorcerer tried to buy the Holy Spirit. Of course, the Holy Spirit is not for sale. He is a free gift from the Father. Yet some Gospel preachers today are still trying to peddle the Holy Spirit. Oh, it's subtle alright. Just remember you can't buy a spiritual breakthrough. If you're in the habit of trying to buy your breakthrough by sowing into ministries with a hyped up prosperity messages that don't line up with the Word of God, stop and repent now. I believe God wants us all to prosper and be in health even as our soul prospers (3 John 1:2). But the Gospel isn't the multi-level marketing scheme as some have made it out to be. Consider Peter's strong words to Simon:

> "To hell with your money! And you
> along with it. Why, that's
> unthinkable—trying to buy God's

gift! You'll never be part of what God is doing by striking bargains and offering bribes. Change your ways—and now! Ask the Master to forgive you for trying to use God to make money. I can see this is an old habit with you; you reek with money-lust."

—Acts 8:20 (The Message)

Again, if you have tapped into the wrong spirit of sowing or reaping, just repent. God is a God of grace. Maybe you did it out of ignorance. Maybe you were even deceived. Just change your ways and be a good steward of God's money, and a good example to God's people, and don't look back.

Vicious Habits

Beyond these bad and evil habits, we find a number of references to vicious and sinful habits to avoid. Let's take a look at a few more, in brief.

Paul talked about the "vicious habit of depersonalizing everyone into a rival: (Galatians 5:19 Message). Competing is fine when you're playing tennis or video games. But I've seen too many Christians competing for things that only God can give them, like gifts, talents and positions. The result is strife and envy. This reminds me of what James wrote in his epistle: "You want what you don't have, so you scheme and kill to get it. You are jealous of what others have, but you can't get it, so you fight and wage war to take it away from them. Yet you don't have what you want because you don't ask God for it" (James 4:2 NLT). Ask the Lord for what you want and trust Him for His timing.

Paul also warned Timothy about the habit of being idle and how it leads to gossip (1 Timothy 5:13 NIV). Gossip betrays (Proverbs 11:13 NIV). King Solomon said, "The words of gossip are like choice morsels; they go down to a man's inmost parts (Proverbs 18:8 NIV). If you are prone to gossip, as the Lord to help you break that habit—and get busy. The busier you are doing the work of the Lord the less time you have to gossip.

The writer of Hebrews talked about how some Christians had, "picked up this bad habit of not listening" (Hebrews 5:11 The Message). That's an especially bad habit, seeing that Jesus said to "Pay attention to how you hear. To those who listen to my teaching, more understanding will be given. But for those who are not listening, even what they think they understand will be taken away from them" (Luke 8:18). No matter who is talking, listen attentively out of respect. The humble heart can learn something from anyone. Be slow to speak and quick to listen (James 1:19).

The writer of Hebrews also warned against the habit of not gathering together with the saints (Hebrews 10:25). It's vital to be plugged into a local church where you can worship, pray, fellowship and serve with those of like precious faith. Iron sharpens iron. God uses our relationships with fellow believers to strengthen us and help us see areas in our lives where we need to grow. No believer is an island unto himself. We need each other.

In Hosea 4:12, the Lord was grieved by the fact that the children of Israel were "habitually asking counsel of their senseless wood idols." An idol is anything that sets itself up in God's place in your life. Who do you consult when you have problems? Your bank account? Your best friend? Or the Living God? Victorious Christian living finds safety in the counsel of many, but not at the expense of leaving the Counselor out of the mix.

Keep in mind that Jesus paid a dear price to give you the right to go boldly to the throne of grace and obtain mercy and find grace to help you in your time of need (Hebrews 4:6). If it wasn't for the blood of Jesus...I don't even want to think about it. Don't slip back into your worldly habits. The Apostle Paul said:

> "All of you, slave and free both, were once held hostage in a sinful society. Then a huge sum was paid

out for your ransom. So please don't, out of old habit, slip back into being or doing what everyone else tells you. Friends, stay where you were called to be. God is there. Hold the high ground with him at your side."

—1 Cor. 7:23 (The Message)

Peter suggested to, "Think of your sufferings as a weaning from that old sinful habit of always expecting to get your own way. Then you'll be able to live out your days free to pursue what God wants instead of being tyrannized by what you want" (1 Peter 4:1). Breaking bad habits may cause some temporary suffering in your soul—or even your flesh—because you aren't getting what you think you want. But you don't really want the fruit of those bad habits. Not really. And the suffering is only temporary. The good habits you develop could set you up for eternal rewards.

Good and Godly Habits

Beyond the *7 Habits of Victorious Christian Living* Paul shared with Timothy, other wise men of God offered some direct insight on godly habits that is worth noting. Let's start with James, the apostle of practical faith.

"And now I have a word for you who brashly announce, 'Today—at the latest, tomorrow—we're off to such and such a city for the year. We're going to start a business and make a lot of money.' You don't know the first thing about tomorrow. You're nothing but a wisp of fog, catching a brief bit of sun before disappearing. Instead, make it a habit to say, 'If the Master wills it and we're still alive, we'll do this or that'."

—James 4:13 (The Message)

Finally, in the Book of Psalms we also find some good and godly habits worth pursuing:

"Everyone sees it. God's work is the talk of the town. Be glad, good people! Fly to God! Good-hearted people, make praise your habit."

—Psalm 64:9 (The Message)

"Hallelujah! Thank God! And why?

> Because he's good, because his love lasts. But who on earth can do it— declaim God's mighty acts, broadcast all his praises? You're one happy man when you do what's right, one happy woman when you form the habit of justice."

—Psalm 106:1 (The Message)

As we close this section, consider this question from a group of Jesus followers. They asked Him, "What are we to do, that we may [habitually] be working the works of God? [What are we to do to carry out what God requires?]" (John 6:28 AMP). What was Jesus' answer? Just believe in Him. Your faith in Christ and your desire to do the works He has planned for you will help you break out of your bad habits and develop good and godly habits. Remember, it's only by His grace that we live and move and have our being (Acts 17:28).

Don't Beat Yourself Up!

Now that we've outlined bad, good and godly habits, let's employ the "out with the old, in with the new" philosophy. Let's determine to put off the old man and put on the new man. Let's work with God break those bad habits and form new ones that will lead us into more victorious

Christian living. The first step to breaking bad habits is not to beat yourself up that you formed them, or even that you are struggling to break them. You can't wallow in the devil's condemnation and bask in God's grace at the same time. I set before you grace and condemnation. Choose grace.

Let the Apostle Paul serve as an encouragement to you:

> "For I do not understand my own actions [I am baffled, bewildered]. I do not practice or accomplish what I wish, but I do the very thing that I loathe [which my moral instinct condemns]. Now if I do [habitually] what is contrary to my desire, [that means that] I acknowledge and agree that the Law is good (morally excellent) and that I take sides with it. However, it is no longer I who do the deed, but the sin [principle] which is at home in me and has possession of me.

> For I know that nothing good dwells within me, that is, in my flesh. I can will what is right, but I cannot perform it. [I have the intention and urge to do what is right, but no power to carry it out.]

For I fail to practice the good deeds I desire to do, but the evil deeds that I do not desire to do are what I am [ever] doing.

Now if I do what I do not desire to do, it is no longer I doing it [it is not myself that acts], but the sin [principle] which dwells within me [fixed and operating in my soul].

So I find it to be a law (rule of action of my being) that when I want to do what is right and good, evil is ever present with me and I am subject to its insistent demands. For I endorse and delight in the Law of God in my inmost self [with my new nature].

But I discern in my bodily members [in the sensitive appetites and wills of the flesh] a different law (rule of action) at war against the law of my mind (my reason) and making me a prisoner to the law of sin that dwells in my bodily organs [in the sensitive appetites and wills of the flesh].

O unhappy and pitiable and wretched man that I am! Who will release and deliver me from [the shackles of] this body of death? O thank God! [He will!] through Jesus Christ (the Anointed One) our Lord!

—Romans 7:15-25 (AMP)

Paul understood the struggle. He understood that the grace of God was stronger than his bad habits. He understood that it was Jesus who would deliver him from ungodly habits. Paul understood that if he agreed with God and yielded to the Holy Spirit, he would be transformed. The same holds true for us. What good does it do to wallow in condemnation when we could be receiving grace, mercy and forgiveness? Our merciful God has this gracious habit of being forgiving, you know? Consider the words of the psalmist: "If you, God, kept records on wrongdoings, who would stand a chance? As it turns out, forgiveness is your habit, and that's why you're worshiped" (Psalm 130:3 The Message).

CHAPTER 11
Rooting Out Bad Habits

See, I have this day set thee over the nations and over the kingdoms, to root out, and to pull down, and to destroy, and to throw down, to build, and to plant.

—Jeremiah 1:10

Are you ready to work with God to break some of the bad habits that are holding you back from living a victorious—or an even more victorious—Christian life? It's important that you make a quality decision and not just nod your head with mental ascent. If you don't make a quality decision, then you won't follow through on the process of breaking bad habits and forming new ones.

Poet James Allen put it this way: "Men are anxious to improve their circumstances, but are unwilling to improve themselves; they therefore remain bound. The man who does not shrink from self-crucifixion can never fail to accomplish the object upon which his heart is set. This is true of earthly as of heavenly things."

OK, I never said it would be easy. But it is possible to break even the ugliest, most sinful habits. The Bible says nothing is impossible with God (Luke 1:37). God is standing by, ready, willing, and available to help you. So without further ado, here are some practical steps for breaking bad habits.

1. Make a quality decision.

You need to make a quality decision. You already know it's God's will for you to break those bad habits. Get into agreement with God's Word and put your stake in the ground of change. Count the costs and the pain of keeping the bad habit, then count the benefits and the pleasures of breaking the bad habit. Compare those lists and the decision will be easier to make.

Once you've made this decision, swear to your own hurt and change not (Psalm 15:4). Refer back to your pain-versus-benefits list if you start to waver. Remember, a double-minded man is unstable in all his ways (James 1:8). Once you've made your decision in faith, take action immediately before the devil has a chance to talk you out of it. Faith without works is dead.

The first action you can take is to be diligent about your thought life. If you haven't already, I would recommend picking up a copy of Joyce Meyer's *Battlefield of the Mind* and *Power Thoughts*.

2. Take control of your thoughts.

Our actions start with our thoughts. So if you are going to break a bad habit, you need to take control of your thoughts. American Minister and Cartoonist Frank A. Clark said, "A habit is something you can do without thinking—which is why most of us have so many of them."

Habits are often lodged in your subconscious mind. But the enemy also works on the battlefield of our conscious mind to introduce suggestions, when, if acted upon, can lead us into the bondage of bad habits—or even worse bondages. British Author Samuel Johnson adequately described the situation when he said, "The chains of habit are generally too small to be felt until they are too strong to be broken."

We need to take control of our own thoughts before the devil forges strongholds in our minds. God is not going to do that part for us. But He has equipped us to do it by His Word and His Spirit. Remember, the enemy is roaming about like a roaring lion, seeking whom he may devour (1 Peter 5:7-8). When the enemy sets his sites on his target, he has to stop long enough to pull back the bow that releases his fiery darts. That gives you enough time to lift up your shield of faith—if you are paying attention to your thoughts.

I believe some of those fiery darts are imaginations; thoughts that work to dictate our actions. Maybe you want to quit smoking cigarettes. Maybe your mouth is the problem. Maybe you need more self-discipline to wake up early and pray. The enemy will give you thoughts that lead you away from that goal rather than toward it. He sends imaginations that, when you receive, believe and act upon them, send your godly intentions up in smoke. The Good News is the Bible tells us what to do with those imaginations: cast them down.

> "For the weapons of our warfare are not carnal, but mighty through God to the pulling down of strong holds;) Casting down imaginations, and every high thing that exalteth itself against the knowledge of God, and bringing into captivity every thought to the obedience of Christ; And having in a readiness to revenge all disobedience, when your obedience is fulfilled."

—2 Corinthians 10:4-6

I like the Message translation of this verse:

> "The tools of our trade aren't for marketing or manipulation, but they are for demolishing that entire massively corrupt culture. We use our powerful God-tools for smashing warped philosophies, tearing down barriers erected against the truth of God, fitting every loose thought and emotion and impulse into the structure of life shaped by Christ. Our tools are ready at hand for clearing the ground of every obstruction and building lives of obedience into maturity."

That's the key: fitting every thought and emotion and impulse into a life shaped by Christ. When you feel the impulse to act on a bad habit, grab that thought, think about what the Word says about it, and speak the truth out of your mouth right then and there. Don't wait a moment. Do it immediately. If you continually do this, you will conquer that bad habit—because it begins with a thought.

3. Renew your mind.

Of course, it gets much easier to capture those devilish thoughts when you've renewed your mind to the Word of God. When you renew your mind, you are replacing wrong beliefs with right beliefs. When you have right beliefs, you'll have right actions because we take action based on our beliefs. If you believe you are bound to bad habits, like anger, because your dad was an angry man, then you won't put up much resistance to the devil—and he won't flee. But if you renew your mind to who you are in Christ, you will resist those temptations because it doesn't line up with your spiritual DNA.

> "I beseech you therefore, brethren, by the mercies of God, that ye present your bodies a living sacrifice, holy, acceptable unto God, which is your reasonable service. And be not conformed to this world: but be ye transformed by the renewing of your mind, that ye may prove what is that good, and acceptable, and perfect, will of God."
>
> —Romans 12:1-2

Bad habits are not the good, and acceptable and perfect will of God. Renewing your mind to

God's Word and God's ways will set the stage for building godly habits. Listen in to the Message translation of these verses from the Book of Romans:

> "So here's what I want you to do, God helping you: Take your everyday, ordinary life—your sleeping, eating, going-to-work, and walking-around life—and place it before God as an offering. Embracing what God does for you is the best thing you can do for him. Don't become so well-adjusted to your culture that you fit into it without even thinking. Instead, fix your attention on God. You'll be changed from the inside out. Readily recognize what he wants from you, and quickly respond to it. Unlike the culture around you, always dragging you down to its level of immaturity, God brings the best out of you, develops well-formed maturity in you."

Wow. That really brings it home doesn't it? Offer your life to God. Embrace what He does for you. Fix your attention on Him. And you'll be changed from the inside out.

We can find one final take on this powerful verse in the Amplified version. Romans 12:2 says to "Be transformed (changed) by the [entire] renewal of your mind [by its new ideals and its new attitude]." You'll find those new ideals in the Word of God. And when you find them, and renew your mind to them, you will have a new attitude—and breaking bad habits will no longer be the monumental struggle it once was. When you continue in the Word, you will know the truth, and the truth will set you free (John 8:32).

4. Write out your new goals every day.

I have a spiral notebook that's reserved for writing out my goals. I write out the same 10 goals every day. It may seem redundant to write out your goals every day, but it's a powerful exercise—and it's Scriptural. Habakkuk 2:2 says, "Write the vision, and make it plain upon tables, that he may run that readeth it."

Don't write your goal to break a habit—or any other goal—in the negative future tense. Write it as if already done; in the positive present tense. So instead of writing, "I will not sleep in late" you would write, "I arise early in the morning to seek His face." Can you see the difference? This enters your subconscious as a direct command and equips your mind to work with you toward reaching that goal. The subconscious mind doesn't process words like "not." So the negative command of, "I will not sleep in late" translates to your subconscious mind as "I will sleep in late." Write out your new, godly habits as already achieved every day and reprogram your subconscious mind. Call those things that be not as though they are (Romans 4:17).

5. Confess the Word of God.

Once you've written down your goals, find Scriptures that back them up and confess them out loud. If you have a habit of getting angry, for example, confess Scriptures about being peaceful and walking in love. If you have a habit of gossiping, confess Scriptures that instruct us about what to do with our mouths—and put it in the first person.

For example, the Bible says, "Don't use foul or abusive language. Let everything you say be good and helpful, so that your words will be an encouragement to those who hear them" (Ephesians 4:29 NLT). If you put that in the first person, positive tense, it would read this way, "Everything I say is good and helpful. My words are an encouragement to those that hear them."

Confessing any portion of Scripture is a good habit to adopt. But confessing Scriptures that deal with your specific challenges—your bad habits and weak points—is a more targeted approach to working with God to bring about the change you both want in your life.

6. Get an accountability partner.

You've heard of prayer partners, right? Well, an accountability partner is similar, except the main purpose of the relationship is not to pray. An accountability partner is a person who coaches another person to keep a commitment. When you have an accountability partner, you both encourage each other to keep making progress toward your goals.

Of course, you can pray with your accountability partner at the end of your call. You can get into agreement that you will both find the grace needed to break bad habits and forge new ones. But this is more than a prayer meeting. This is a relationship that holds you to your word. If you say you are going to meditate on peace Scriptures this week, your accountability partner will follow up with you to make sure you did, find out why you didn't if you didn't, and encourage you to get back on track next week.

We all need people who we can trust and to whom we can hold ourselves accountable. Choose and be an accountability partner who is quick to listen, slow to speak, and slow to become angry (James 1:19). Choose and be an accountability partner who is not judgmental. Choose and be an accountability partner who is compassionate and loving. And also choose and be an accountability partner who is serious about getting results.

7. Use your holy imagination.

God gave you an imagination. It's OK to use it. In fact, God expects you to use it. That's why He gave it to you. Our imagination is the part of our mind where we can visualize something that has not yet manifested in the natural. The Holy Spirit can communicate with us through our imagination.

Use your holy imagination to visualize yourself as having conquered the bad habit and exercising the new one. If you smoke cigarettes with your coffee, picture yourself drinking coffee without smoking cigarettes. If you have a bad habit of parking in front of the television for hours every night, visualize yourself taking a walk, studying the Word, or spending quality time with your family instead.

Don't let the New Age movement steal visualization from you. God gave you your imagination. So long as you use it to imagine things that are in line with His Word, you are using it in a righteous way. Think about Scriptures, for example, and see yourself walking in those Scriptures. Maybe you've struggled with a bad habit for a long time and you think it's impossible to break it. Seeing the impossible makes it possible. If you can see it, you can have it.

French philosopher Jules de Gaultier said, "Imagination is the one weapon in the war against reality." Your holy imagination can be a weapon in the war against the reality of your bad habits. The devil likes to use or imaginations against us, bringing fear and other negative emotions to our souls in order to dictate our actions. Take back your imagination and begin to visualize yourself the way Jesus sees you, with everything Jesus died to give you.

8. Focus on one bad habit at a time.

Don't try to tackle every bad habit you have at once. Wisdom dictates being diligent and focused in one area until you conquer it. Alexander Graham Bell, the American inventor who brought us the telephone, said this: "Concentrate all your thoughts upon the work at hand. The sun's rays do not burn until brought to a focus." When you focus on defeating one bad habit—when you shine the light of God's grace on that one area—you will see results more quickly than if you try to take the mountain of bad habits all at once.

And don't focus on the problem, focus on the solution. Abraham didn't focus on his own impotence and say, "It's hopeless. This hundred-year-old body could never father a child. Nor did he survey Sarah's decades of infertility and give up (Romans 4:19 The Message). Abraham focused on the promise of God. You should do the same. The Word never fails. If you apply the Word to your situation with steady pressure, you will eventually see the breakthrough into a new level of victorious Christian living.

9. Do an evening review.

Every evening before you go to bed, review the day. Look for areas where you stumbled back into the bad habit you are working to break. If you can see the pattern, you can stop the pattern by the grace of God. Also, encourage yourself by looking for areas where you reigned victorious over that bad habit. By taking just five minutes to look back over the day, you can see where you went right and where you went wrong, then ask God to help you do better tomorrow.

10. Keep an attitude of gratitude.

As you continue on your journey of breaking bad habits, keep an attitude of gratitude. Be thankful that God is with you on the journey. He is the one empowering you to overcome those dark habits.

> "Work out (cultivate, carry out to the goal, and fully complete) your own salvation with reverence and awe and trembling (self-distrust, with serious caution, tenderness of

conscience, watchfulness against temptation, timidly shrinking from whatever might offend God and discredit the name of Christ).

[Not in your own strength] for it is God Who is all the while effectually at work in you [energizing and creating in you the power and desire], both to will and to work for His good pleasure and satisfaction and delight."

—Philippians 2:12-13 (AMP)

It's His good pleasure to help you break bad habits and forge new ones. Thank Him every step along the way, even when you stumble. Be confident that He who began a good work in you will carry it on to completion until the day of Christ Jesus (Philippians 1:6).

11. Refuse to give up.

Jesus wasn't a quitter. And you aren't either. You might feel like quitting, especially if the battle against your mind has been raging for a while and you aren't seeing any sign of breakthrough. When you feel like giving up, you don't want to hear any more clichés about the light at the end of the tunnel or how it's always darkest before the dawn. This is where an accountability partner can work to encourage you. But you also have to determine in your own heart not to give up. You have to do like David did: Encourage yourself in the Lord.

American Inventor Thomas Edison was certain that, "Our greatest weakness lies in giving up. The most certain way to succeed is always to try just one more time." An unknown wise man took that a step further, saying, "Defeat may test you; it need not stop you. If at first you don't succeed, try another way. For every obstacle there is a solution. Nothing in the world can take the place of persistence. The greatest mistake is giving up."

The Bible has plenty to say about perseverance. You have need of endurance, so that when you have done the will of God you can receive what is promised (Hebrews 10:36). And again, "Let us not grow weary in doing good, for in due season we will reap if we do not give up" (Galatians 6:9). You can do it!

12. Give the glory to God.

When you break that bad habit, be sure to give all the glory to God. Without Him, we can do nothing. Yes, it was our decision to try to break the habit—and His grace was sufficient. But we shouldn't think more highly of ourselves than we ought (Romans 12:3). Let this be your confession, "Thanks be to God, who always leads us in triumphal procession in Christ and through us spreads everywhere the fragrance of the knowledge of him" (2 Corinthians 2:14).

Developing Godly Habits

You can't just sweep the house clean of your bad habits. You've got to fill that space with good habits or the bad habits will be more likely to creep back in. Again, you need to make a quality decision and rely on the power of the Holy Spirit. You can follow most of the same steps in the last section to form good habits. Actually, you should try to introduce the good as a substitute for the bad as you go through the process of transformation by the grace of God.

Maxwell Maltz, a U.S. plastic surgeon and motivational author, said this: "One of the reasons it has seemed so difficult for a person to change his habits, his personality, or his way of life, has been that heretofore nearly all efforts at change have been directed to the circumference of the self, so to speak, rather than to the center."

What I take away from that is this: all permanent changes begins in our spirit, not in our soul. Yes, will power can take us a long way, but will power alone won't take us all the way to the finish line to which Paul raced. Remember what Paul said to the Galatians:

"But I say, walk and live [habitually] in the [Holy] Spirit [responsive to and controlled and guided by the Spirit]; then you will certainly not gratify the cravings and desires of the flesh (of human nature without God)."

—Galatians 5:16 (AMP)

Victorious Christian living is living out of our spirits, by the leading of the Holy Spirit, with a mind, will and emotions submitted to Him. This requires the grace of God. And Paul knew this. In the final words of his final epistle, Paul left his dear spiritual son with these words:

"The Lord Jesus Christ be with thy spirit. Grace be with you. Amen" (2 Timothy 4:22).

And those are my words to you, my friend. The Lord Jesus Christ is with your spirit. I pray that you exercise your faith to receive the grace that's available to you to live a victorious Christian life. Amen!

BREAKTHROUGH!

CONCLUSION

As I close out this volume of work, I'm reminded of the Book of Ecclesiastes. I remember the first time I read it. Solomon was on a quest to find happiness—and so was I. Along the way, he comes across vanity after vanity after vanity before coming to a final conclusion: fear God and do what He tells you.

> "All has been heard; the end of the matter is: Fear God [revere and worship Him, knowing that He is] and keep His commandments, for this is the whole of man [the full, original purpose of his creation, the object of God's providence, the root of character, the foundation of all happiness, the adjustment to all inharmonious circumstances and conditions under the sun] and the whole [duty] for every man."

> —Ecclesiastes 8:13 (AMP)

The bottom line with the *7 Habits of Victorious Christian Living* is found right here in this verse. If we respect God and if we surrender to His will, we will avoid the snares of bad habits and establish not just good habits, but godly habits that set the stage for victory in every area of our lives. It's just that simple. Of course, it's not as easy as it is simple. That's why I wrote this book—to break down into practical steps how we can live in victory. It takes discipline. It takes a heart after God. And it takes His grace—for apart from Him we can't even walk in His will.

Let's pray:

Father, in the name of Jesus, I thank you that you are with me. I thank you that you will never leave or forsake me. I thank you that you know all of my bad habits—and you love me anyway. Nothing can separate me from the love of God that is in Christ Jesus—not even my bad habits.

Lord, I ask you to forgive me of my sinful thoughts, attitudes, words and actions. Cleanse me with the blood of Jesus. Create in my a clean heart and renew a right spirit within me and help me. Help me Lord, to break every bad habit that has held me in bondage to the world's system. Help me Lord to persevere by your grace to take control of my thoughts, renew my mind and walk in your Word. Help me Lord to form godly habits that glorify your name.

Father, I thank you that you've heard my prayer. And I know that if since you've heard me, I have what I have asked of you. So right now, I receive your forgiveness. I receive your mercy. I receive your grace to break bad habits and form new ones that will position me to see your promises come to full manifestation in my life.

In Jesus' name I pray. Amen and amen.

ABOUT THE AUTHOR

Jennifer LeClaire is a prophetic voice and teacher whose passion is to see the lost come to Christ and equip believers to understand the will and ways of God. She carries a reforming voice that seeks to turn hearts to the Lord and edify the Body of Christ.

Jennifer has a powerful testimony of God's power to set the captives free and claim beauty for ashes. She shares her story with women who need to understand the love and grace of God in a lost and dying world.

Jennifer is news editor at Charisma magazine, as well as a prolific author who has written several books, including "The Heart of the Prophetic," "A Prophet's Heart," "Doubtless: Faith that Overcomes the World," and "Fervent Faith: Discover how a fervent spirit is a defense against the devil." Her materials have been translated into several languages. Some of her work is archived in the Flower Pentecostal Heritage Museum.

Other Books by Jennifer LeClaire

The Heart of the Prophetic: Keys to flowing in a more powerful prophetic anointing

Doubtless: Faith that Overcomes the World

Fervent Faith: Discover how a fervent spirit is a defense against the devil.

A Prophet's Heart: Avoiding the Doorway to Deception

27 Ways to Judge Prophecy

Visit Jennifer online at:

www.jenniferleclaire.org

www.facebook.com/propheticbooks

www.twitter.com/propheticbooks

www.youtube.com/jnleclaire

www.flickr.com/propheticbooks

www.myspace.com/propheticbooks

www.connect.tangle.com/propheticbooks

CPSIA information can be obtained
at www.ICGtesting.com
Printed in the USA
FSOW01n0519250816
23971FS